Current Trends in Islamist Ideology

VOLUME 12

Edited by
Hillel Fradkin,
Husain Haqqani (on leave),
Eric Brown,
and Hassan Mneimneh

HUDSON INSTITUTE

Center on Islam, Democracy, and the Future of the Muslim World

For more information about obtaining additional copies of this or other Hudson Institute publications, please visit Hudson's website at **www.hudson.org/bookstore or call toll free: 1-888-554-1325**.

ABOUT HUDSON INSTITUTE

Hudson Institute is a nonpartisan, independent policy research organization dedicated to innovative research and analysis that promotes global security, prosperity, and freedom. Founded in 1961 by strategist Herman Kahn, Hudson Institute challenges conventional thinking and helps manage strategic transitions to the future through interdisciplinary studies in defense, international relations, economics, health care, technology, culture, and law. With offices in Washington and New York, Hudson seeks to guide public policymakers and global leaders in government and business through a vigorous program of publications, conferences, policy briefings, and recommendations. Hudson Institute is a 501(c)(3) organization financed by tax-deductible contributions from private individuals, corporations, foundations, and by government grants.

Visit **www.hudson.org** for more information.

ABOUT THE CENTER ON ISLAM, DEMOCRACY, AND THE FUTURE OF THE MUSLIM WORLD

Hudson Institute's Center on Islam conducts a wide-ranging program of research and analysis addressed to the political, religious, social, and other dynamics within majority Muslim countries and Muslim populations around the world. A principal focus of the Center's work is the ideological dynamic within Islam and the connected issue of how this political and religious debate impacts both Islamic radicalism and the Muslim search for moderate and democratic alternatives. Through its research, which includes collaboration with partners throughout the Muslim world and elsewhere, the Center aims to contribute to the development of effective policy options and strategies to win the worldwide struggle against radical Islam.

For more information, visit **www.CurrentTrends.org**

Contents

Egypt's Muslim Brotherhood After the Revolution

By Samuel Tadros

THE EXTRAORDINARY SCENES BROADCASTED FROM TAHRIR SQUARE IN Cairo during the eighteen days that led to the fall of Hosni Mubarak in February, 2011, were met with great enthusiasm and support in Western countries. Politicians and numerous scholars were hopeful that the revolution, with the young liberals who were portrayed as leading it, would lead to a better future for Egyptians. They were also hopeful that Egypt's politics would finally break free from the struggle between dictatorial regimes and Islamists that has paralyzed the country as well as the modern politics of other countries in the Arab world. Finally, the gridlock was broken and the blossoms of the Arab Spring were flourishing.

Contrary to initial hopes, however, the role of Islamists has not regressed; indeed, seven months after the revolutionary euphoria wore off, the Muslim Brotherhood remains at the forefront of Egyptian politics. In fact, the erosion of the state's security apparatus gave Islamists an unprecedented opportunity to shape the country's political debate. With elections now scheduled for a parliament that will form a constitution writing committee, many have begun to fear that the Islamists will not be merely one among many actors on Egypt's new political scene. Instead, many fear that we may face a future when Islamists write the rules of Egypt's new politics, putting their long-term mark on the new system to ensure their continued control.

The Muslim Brotherhood is at the center of the current struggle to shape Egypt's future. Since the Egyptian Muslim Brotherhood is the mother organization of Arab Islamism, the ramifications of the struggle in Egypt are likely to spill over to other countries in the region. For years, a fierce debate has taken place among Western scholars regarding the Brotherhood. Has the Brotherhood—which began in 1928 as a reactionary and sometimes violent ideological movement bent on constructing an Islamic State—changed its approach to politics and its principles? Should the United States open a dialogue with them? While some have argued that the Brotherhood has become moderate and have portrayed it as a socially conservative movement committed to democracy,[1] others have warned that the Brotherhood's declarations on their commitment to democratic rule were a sign not of moderation but of pragmatism. The Brotherhood's objectives had not, in fact, changed since its founding. What had changed was the movement's overall ability to achieve its objectives as well as its ability to project and frame this project (especially in English) in a way that would win the sympathy of outsiders. Given the opportunity, the Brotherhood would seek to implement its long-term radical agenda to establish an Islamic State.

That opportunity has arrived. The breakdown of the state's security apparatus and the opening in the political system has given the Brotherhood an historical chance to operate freely and position itself as the strongest player in a new Egypt. While several constraints on its power remain, the most obvious of which is the Egyptian armed forces, the Brotherhood's newly acquired freedom of action has meant a new self-confidence in its strength and an increased willingness to elaborate more clearly and publicly on the kind of new society the Brotherhood aims to build. The new freedom has, however, not come without new challenges for the Brotherhood. Since the revolution, the Brotherhood's leadership has been preoccupied with questions of how to retain the movement's youth membership, how to structure its relationship with both the newly established Freedom and Justice Party (FJP) and the armed forces, and how the Brotherhood as a whole should deal with a changing and volatile political environment. Examining how the Brotherhood has shaped and been in turn affected by Egypt's changing political environment helps us understand not only how the Brotherhood operates but also, more importantly, how it thinks.

The Revolution Surprise

THE SUCCESS OF THE DEMONSTRATORS IN EGYPT IN ENDING THE THIRTY-YEAR RULE of Hosni Mubarak surprised the world. What seemed like a stable authoritarian grip on power was brought to its knees in just a few days. Perhaps no one was more surprised than the Egyptians themselves—especially the Muslim Brotherhood. This explains, in part, the Brotherhood's statements describing the revolution as a "work of God,"[2] as no human action could fully explain for them what had taken place.

The Brotherhood's political position in the days leading up to the Egyptian revolution was weak. Its parliamentary success in the 2005 elections was not matched in the elections of 2010. Due to substantial state intervention and vote rigging, the Brotherhood did not win a single seat in the first round of elections and had only twenty-seven members competing in the second round.[3] Faced with a crushing defeat, the Brotherhood decided to boycott the second round. While state intervention certainly played a role, the Brotherhood had already been declining politically during the previous five years. Its financial arm had been crushed by the money laundering trials of Deputy General Guide Khairat al-Shater and Hassan Malik, a prominent Brotherhood businessman. The state's targeted prosecution of these Brotherhood businessmen resulted in harsh verdicts and the confiscation of their companies.[4] Furthermore, the Brotherhood MPs that came to power in 2005 had not delivered on much of their promises during their five-year terms. Frustrations were mounting inside the Brotherhood's youth wing, which saw the movement as incapable of taking a bold stand against the regime. The movement was also plagued by internal conflicts that resulted in the removal of Mohamed Habib, the Deputy General Guide, and Abdel Moneim Aboul Fetouh from the Guidance Council. The Brotherhood's predicament was evident when one of its MPs, Magdy Ashour, decided to ignore the leadership's decisions and run in the second round anyway. Accusations that the Brotherhood was attempting to kidnap Ashour to force him to comply were not helpful to the movement's public image.[5]

When calls for a demonstration against the government started to circulate on the Internet and elsewhere on January 25, 2011, the Brotherhood initially did not think it would garner much public support. Calls from political entities and figures with no significant grassroots following would likely only result in the usual small-size demonstrations by the usual familiar faces. For an organization like the Brotherhood that had grown accustomed to the state's repression, the idea that the regime could be brought down through protest was absurd. It is true that Tunisia inspired hope, for some more than others, but the passing of time, not to mention old age, had taught the Brotherhood's leadership to be cautious. Experience also taught them that the Islamist movement would likely end up paying the heaviest price, in the form of arrests and torture, should the state crack down on public demonstrations.

Yet, as the day of protest approached, growing pressure by younger Brotherhood members, combined with the fact that even long-established political parties not known for street activism, such as Al Wafd, decided they would join the demonstrations, the Brotherhood leadership decided to take the middle path that would please everyone. On January 23, 2011, the Brotherhood announced it would take part in the demonstrations.[6] It sought to portray the Brotherhood as part of the rest of the Egyptian opposition and as a movement not distant from popular demands—a position and public image it always sought. Furthermore, the leadership gave a green light to young members to join the demonstrations. What the declaration did not mean, however, was that the Brotherhood would actually mobilize its members and join the protests with the movement's full power. Thus, during the first two days of demonstrations, the movement was not rallied or organized and one could not see the Brotherhood descending in mass numbers onto Tahrir square.

After being surprised by the rapid increase in the number of protestors (which, while still small, exceeded the size of usual demonstrations), the Brotherhood began to sense an opportunity. They calculated that the regime was much weaker than it was previously thought to be—a reality that became increasingly evident with the government's internet and mobile phone ban. The next demonstration, which was scheduled for Friday 28, 2011, was an ideal setting for the Brotherhood to show its power. After Friday prayers, the movement began mobilizing its members, and, by using each mosque as a launching site for a demonstration, the Brotherhood was able to pour an enormous amount of people onto the streets. The results were spectacular. In a few hours the police force was being hammered. Contrary to earlier exaggerated estimations of the strength of the Egyptian police, the police force in Cairo was a mere 17,000 strong.[7] Under siege from every corner, the moment of collapse took place when 99 police stations across the country were attacked. The only solution for the regime was to call in the army.

The Worst Nightmare?

UNLIKE THE YOUTHFUL DEMONSTRATORS WHO CHANTED "THE ARMY AND THE people are one hand," the Brotherhood understood better. Shaped by their earlier experience in 1954 when the army brutally suppressed them, the Brotherhood understood clearly that the army they were now facing was the real core of the regime, unencumbered by its outer layers. But the Brotherhood, as well as the public at large, had little knowledge of the army's political intentions in this new situation. Simply put, there was little information publicly available about the army, and no one knew exactly who was calling the shots. When Mubarak appointed Omar Suleiman as Vice President the next day, the Brotherhood naturally concluded that he was the army's man. It is with this in mind that they agreed to enter into a dialogue with Suleiman, despite the fact that other movements chose to boycott such meetings[8] and despite all the indications of the personal hatred that Suleiman felt towards the Islamists. These calculations persisted for some time with the Brotherhood's leadership professing to have no objections to Omar Suleiman becoming president of the country, as he was untainted by the Mubarak regime.[9]

In the early phases of the revolution, the Brotherhood's goals were straightforward. Still unsure of whether the regime would fall, though well aware of the government's vulnerabilities, the movement aimed at extracting several key concessions. The first goal was recognition. It was no longer acceptable for the regime to deal with the Brotherhood as if it did not exist; it demanded to be treated as an equal player that had a seat at the table. An official invitation to dialogue with government officials and a change in their status as a "banned group" were essential first steps. Secondly, the Brotherhood demanded permission to form a political party. Thirdly, the Brotherhood aimed to ensure that it would not be excluded from politics in the future. It therefore focused its efforts on changing the constitutional clauses dealing with presidential nominations.

The Brotherhood was, however, careful not to overplay its hand. The movement's leadership deeply feared a backlash, which they thought likely, especially if the regime was able to convince the West and the U.S. in particular that the Islamist threat loomed and had to be crushed. While plausible, the fear within the movement was also built on a conspiracy-driven mindset and on a distorted view of reality. The Brotherhood, like many other opposition groups, saw the relationship between the U.S. and the Egyptian regime as one of a superpower and a local client. Believing in all sorts of conspiracy theories, the Brotherhood has always exaggerated the U.S.'s influence over Mubarak and the army. This is one reason why the Brotherhood has sought to moderate its message in English. During the revolution, the Brotherhood sought to assuage fears in the West and in the army, too, by indicating their lack of interest in acquiring the Office of the Presidency and by committing to run for only thirty percent of the seats in parliament. More importantly, these assurances were stressed on the ground by attempts to downplay the Brotherhood's role in the revolution.[10] As long as the Brotherhood could reinforce this belief that the Islamists were not behind the uprising (or at least were not its most powerful force) and could keep a low profile, then it could be assured that the movement would raise no red flags in the Western press.

With Mubarak's resignation and his decision to hand over power to the armed forces, it seemed that after fifty-eight years Egypt had come full circle. Bolstered by popular support, the army was again in full control of the country. The façade of civilian rule that had been maintained since 1967 was shattered. For the Brotherhood, what mattered now was avoiding a repeat of 1954, when the army cracked down on Islamists. While well aware that its long-term interests and vision for Egypt were different than the military's, the Brotherhood developed a short-term plan that aimed to appease the military and ensure that a clash does not take place.

Acting Responsibly

THE BROTHERHOOD'S LEADERSHIP ACCURATELY UNDERSTOOD THE MILITARY'S SHORT-term objectives. The military, while not intending to give up its special and privileged position, had no desire to govern Egypt. After Egypt's defeat in the 1967 war, the military recognized that its public image as well as its military preparedness had been adversely affected by its involvement in the daily governing of the country. The military's solution to this was to withdraw from the public spotlight while maintaining overall control over the country. This formula came to an end on February 11, 2011, as the military was forced to govern Egypt. Neither interested nor prepared for the task of daily governance, the military wanted out as soon as possible. Every day it spent dealing with workers' strikes or sectarian clashes decreased their public support and put their real economic interests at risk. The military's objectives have thus been to maintain stability, to ensure economic success in Egypt, and to hand over power to civilian politicians as soon as possible to let them deal with the unsolvable problems.

The military's short-term goals have suited the Brotherhood well. A prolonged transition to civilian rule might lead to Western pressure on the military to stop Islamists. A prolonged transition would also mean further scrutiny by the press and the elite of the Brotherhood's intentions. Similarly, instability might force the military to remain in power. To avoid all those scenarios and the possibility of a clash, the Brotherhood decided to act responsibly. Demands by other groups were not endorsed unless they could clearly serve the Brotherhood's overall interests. Street demonstrations were not joined unless the military could be pressured on a key Brotherhood demand.

The result was an image of the responsible and patriotic partner that the military could talk to. Unlike the disorganized and demagogic protestor groups, the Brotherhood gave the military every reason to prefer talking to them. In addition to the sheer differences in popular support that the Brotherhood enjoyed over the other groups, it had a clear organizational and leader-follower structure. If the army needed to negotiate with political groups, the Brotherhood was the ideal partner. The army could know who to speak to and be assured that once a guarantee is given, the members would abide by the leadership's decisions—something that was not true of the other groups. Furthermore, by refraining from criticizing the military and not participating in demonstrations against the military's leadership, the Brotherhood sought to send a clear message: "we are much more reasonable and pragmatic than you might think, and certainly more than the others." The clearest example of this came when several low-ranking army officers joined the demonstrators on April 8, 2011 and renounced the army's leadership while reading what they called "The First Communiqué." The Brotherhood was quick to withdraw from the scene on that day and leave those men to their fate.

The army for its part did not publicly reveal its worries about the Brotherhood. The key difference between 1954 and today is the army's lack of a political program. Simply put, there is neither a Nasser nor a Nasserism that has emerged inside the army. The army was quick to form a constitutional committee that included one Brotherhood member and that was also chaired by a known Islamist. The committee's resulting document, which endorsed first holding parliamentary elections and then writing a new constitution followed by a presidential election, was exactly what the Brotherhood wanted. The battle for the referendum over the committee's document pitted the Islamists, the military, and the Egyptians who were fed up with the continued uncertainty, against the "liberal" elite. The result was an overwhelming defeat of the latter. While this success gave the Brotherhood further confidence in its strengths compared to other parties, it has also come with complications.

Never Be Alone

FOR THE BROTHERHOOD, POLITICS IN EGYPT IS A GAME OF THREE PLAYERS—ITSELF, THE military, and the "liberal" elite. The three players are not equal in power, but the game remains one in which each has significant chips. In the Brotherhood's eyes, it represents the majority of the people; the army obviously has the guns. The elite deserve more elaboration. Hardly liberal in ideology or discourse, they are an amalgam of diverse groups whose only common denominator is the fact that they are not Islamists. They thus include Christians, Nasserites, Socialists, Trotskyites, businessmen, and a portion of the upper middle class. The only thing uniting this combination of contradictory groups is their fear of the Islamists. As a result, they have traditionally run to the state for protection from the Islamist threat, as was the case during the Islamic terrorist campaign in Egypt during the 1980s and 1990s. Their strength according to the Brotherhood is in their control of the cultural institutions and media of the country.

The political game is thus simple. If two of the three players join forces, the third player loses. This situation has always been the Brotherhood's greatest fear: that non-Islamists would reach a deal with the military on the grounds that both, according to the Brotherhood, have an American patron and that the Islamists would ultimately pay the price and be repressed. So, while the first goal of the Brotherhood since the revolution has been to appease the army, the second most important concern has been to prevent an army alliance with the non-Islamists.

In the years before the revolution, the Brotherhood invested wisely in building bridges with non-Islamists. By showing a face of moderation on some issues and by cooperating with non-Islamists on various ventures against Mubarak, the Brotherhood has been able to allay some elite fears over its agenda. As a result, in most cases it has been non-Islamists who have been spinning the Brotherhood's record and agenda and presenting it as a moderate organization to the Western media. For example, Mohamed El Baradei in an interview with Fareed Zakaria on CNN described the movement as "having nothing to do with extremism," "a minority amongst Egyptians," "in favor of a secular state," and just "a socially conservative group" that is "in favor of every Egyptian having the same rights."[11]

The Brotherhood is thus determined to strike a careful balance and maintain its own links with the non-Islamists. And yet, with the danger of an alliance between the army and non-Islamists in mind, and even though the Brotherhood enjoyed what it interpreted as its resounding victory in the referendum, the Brotherhood has remained fearful of an open struggle breaking out between Islamists and non-Islamists. Should battle lines be drawn, no matter the pragmatism that the Brotherhood shows, there is no guarantee that the army would not betray them. The ideal solution for the Brotherhood, then, is to be part of a grand coalition that would include it and some of the non-Islamist parties.

The Salafist Challenge

WHILE THE MUSLIM BROTHERHOOD IS THE STRONGEST AND MOST POPULAR ISLAMIST group in Egypt, it is hardly the only one. The fall of Mubarak ushered in a new era of freedom for Islamists, and thus we see a proliferation of new Islamist actors and parties. Two major groups—the Salafis and the jihadists, including Jamaa Islamia and Egyptian Islamic Jihad—have resurfaced since the revolution. While both groups have been around for a long time, their acceptance in politics today is entirely a result of the revolution.

The Salafis represent the more important of these two groups politically, and they have built broad-based grassroots networks throughout the country, especially in the countryside and the city of Alexandria. While the Salafis were divided among numerous shaykhs during Mubarak's era and barred from forming umbrella organizations or networks, they managed to quickly unite after the revolution. Long suppressed, and with no knowledge of how politics are conducted, they burst onto the scene like an angry bull. So far, two Salafi parties have emerged as a result: Al Noor (The Light) and Al Asala (Authenticity).

The second Islamist group to re-emerge since the revolution shares most of the Salafi ideology, but it is differentiated by its unique historical experience with formal terrorism. Members of Jamaa Islamia and Egyptian Islamic Jihad, long imprisoned for their roles in the assassination of President Anwar Sadat in 1981 and the subsequent years of Islamist terror, have been freed since the revolution and have suddenly, just like the Salafis, seen the virtues and benefits of the electoral process. After quickly removing the leadership that had brokered a deal with the regime and renounced violence, the names and faces of Abboud al-Zomor, Tarek al-Zomor, and even Mohamed al-Zawahiri returned to haunt the Egyptians. Their political party, Al Bena'a wel Tanmeya (Construction and Development), was rejected by the Parties Committee.[12] The removed "moderate" leadership is setting up its own party named Al Dia'a (Luminance).[13]

The rise of the Salafis and jihadists as a political force has posed a serious challenge to the Muslim Brotherhood. Because the Brotherhood has long been accustomed to being the sole Islamist group competing in elections, the new competitors are sure to complicate things. More importantly, the more extreme views of the Salafis could pull some Brotherhood members toward their flashier rhetoric. In a competition over who is more Islamic, the more extreme groups will win. That is one battle the Brotherhood has no interest in fighting. Furthermore, the media attention given to the Salafi and jihadist groups has proven embarrassing for the Islamist cause. With the Salafis obsessing over Christian women, whom they claim converted to Islam and were kidnapped by the Church,[14] and the weekly jihadist rallies in front of the American Embassy demanding the release of the infamous Blind Shaykh Omar Abdel Rahman,[15] the Brotherhood has become increasingly worried that this Islamist activism will alienate the non-Islamists, the army, and their Western supporters.

To make matters more complex, despite the Brotherhood's pledge to not run for the presidency, there are three announced Islamist candidates. The first, Abdel Moneim Aboul Fetouh, is a former Brotherhood leader, often described in the Western press as a moderate. His decision to run for the presidency against the leadership's wishes has created internal tensions in the movement, since many members do not understand why, considering the fall of the tyrant Mubarak, the movement should be cautious and concede political ground to non-Islamists by not running for president. The second declared Islamist is Selim El Awwa, a member of the Brotherhood splinter party Al Wasat (The Center). A respected Islamic figure by many, he poses similar challenges to the internal cohesion of the movement to Aboul Fetouh. Those two, however, pale in comparison to the threat posed by Hazem Salah Abu Ismail.[16] Abu Ismail, whose father was a leading Islamist and who has already run twice before as a Brotherhood candidate in Egypt's parliamentary elections, represents the largest problem for the Brotherhood. His Islamist bona fides are beyond debate, his dress and manner are modern, and his ideas are appealing to both Brotherhood and Salafi Islamists.

The Salafis' annoying behavior reached its maximum with the demonstrations on July 29, 2011. The Brotherhood's decision to participate in the protests that day was driven by its desire to show the mass support it has and enjoys. The military needed to be reminded of who really controlled the streets. While the Brotherhood and the Salafis had both reached an agreement with the non-Islamist parties beforehand on making the day one of national unity and also on their political demands, the Salafis' political naivety and anger was soon out of control. Frustrated by what they perceived as an attack on Islam by the non-Islamists' insistence on writing a constitution before elections, the hundreds of thousands of Salafis who pooled into Tahrir Square were unapologetic in their Islamist sloganeering. Even Brotherhood members were hard to find in the seas of angry Salafis.[17] The day resulted in the Brotherhood's worst nightmare: the non-Islamists became frightened.

The Grand Coalition

THE MAGIC SOLUTION TO THE BROTHERHOOD'S PROBLEMS LIES IN THE NEXT ELECTIONS. While limiting its candidates to only fifty percent of the seats might seem to be a huge sacrifice from a movement whose long-term agenda is to bring about the total transformation of society along Islamic lines, in reality, the self-imposed limitation serves numerous Brotherhood goals. Winning a comfortable forty percent, for instance, would mean that the Brotherhood would be the most important parliamentary player that no one could ignore. At the same time, such a win would not tie the Brotherhood's hands by forcing it to form a government. Some assume that the Brotherhood is not hungry for power, but this is an incorrect assumption—it is. However, the Brotherhood's ideal situation would be to become part of a governing coalition that insulates the group from being blamed for all the failures that the new government will inevitably face as it grapples with the country's profound economic and other problems. The question for the Brotherhood is therefore "Whom should we partner with?"

Building an electoral coalition to contest the next elections serves a number of purposes for the Brotherhood. First, the non-Brotherhood candidates winning on the joint list will be indebted to the Brotherhood for their victory, and this, in turn, will give the Brotherhood a certain degree of leverage over them. Secondly, if the group has already limited itself to less than fifty percent of the seats (as the Brotherhood has), why not insure that the other fifty percent are friends and not foes? Thirdly, by entering into a coalition with non-Islamists, the Brotherhood seeks to ensure that they are not politically isolated and are able to stop the emergence of an army alliance with non-Islamists. The more the coalition is an amalgam that makes no sense, the better, as this will effectively prohibit the coalition partners from combining against the Brotherhood. This helps to explain why the Brotherhood on June 13, 2011 created the Democratic Alliance for Egypt, along with Al Wafd, Al Ghad, the Nasserite Party, and another thirty smaller parties.[18]

This alliance is popularly portrayed as being against the remnants of the old regime.[19] There is truth to that claim, as the local politicians who sued to win, as National Democratic Party candidates, are the only real competitors to the Brotherhood. But it also serves a more important purpose: balancing. If the alliance included only non-Islamists it would be relentlessly attacked by the Salafis, and the Brotherhood would risk being outflanked by them. By attempting to include them with the non-Islamists, the Brotherhood achieves all its goals in one strike. The Brotherhood will play the role of moderator and middleman between both camps, toning down each side's demands and threatening them from the other side. This strategy was complicated when the Salafi Al Noor Party left the alliance seeking a purer Islamist coalition, though the alliance still includes smaller Islamist groups.

Challenges Within

ISLAMISM'S NEWLY ACQUIRED FREEDOM OF ACTION AS A RESULT OF THE REVOLUTION comes with its own internal problems for the Brotherhood. Many analysts initially had high hopes that the Arab Spring would exacerbate splits inside the movement. Their arguments were based upon the presumed existence of a moderate versus extremist battle over the soul of the Brotherhood, as well as a presumed split within the movement between its youth wing and an older generation that has been reluctant to adapt to changing times. Both arguments have exaggerated the extent of the differences inside the Brotherhood and, more importantly, the ability of any potential breakaway group to pose a threat to the mother organization.

In the mid-1990s, a similar process had taken place with the creation of the Al Wasat Party. The inability of Al Wasat to pose a real threat to the Brotherhood and to pull its members away should have been an educational moment for analysts. Membership in the Brotherhood is a very long process designed to ensure with absolute certainty that there is conformity to the movement's ideology and a clear adherence to its leadership's authority.[20] The ties that exist between Brotherhood members are simply too hard to break. They not only revolve around an ideological agreement, but they also often involve financial, social, as well as family ties. Leaving the movement on bad terms often means losing financially and being shunned by family and friends. The predicament of Aboul Fetouh today serves as an especially telling example. Shunned by his former colleagues (who describe him as having "violated his covenant with God"[21]) and with his campaign banners constantly vandalized by Brotherhood activists, Fetouh is left to criticize the movement[22] but with no effective political ability to offer an alternative. This, however, does not mean that some young members will not leave the movement; some have already left, and some no doubt will continue to do so. But the hope that these defections of individuals could produce a more moderate movement over time is most likely misplaced.[23]

Over the long term, an even more challenging question for the Brotherhood concerns its relationship with its own creation, the Freedom and Justice Party. While the establishment of a political party has been one of the key demands of the movement for years, no elaboration has ever been given on how the movement and the party will ultimately coincide. Now that the movement has a party, such questions have only increased. Could a non-Brotherhood member join the FJP? If he could, could he rise in its leadership? Would some members of the movement remain outside the party? Those kinds of questions remain unanswered. More importantly, the room for action and the party's freedom of decision-making remain unclear. The question of the Brotherhood and the FJP's relationship is in a certain sense not entirely new, as the debate over the political versus social and religious roles of the movement has been raging for years.

The Vision for Egypt

AFTER OFFICIALLY FORMING THE FJP IN FEBRUARY 2011, THE BROTHERHOOD WAS forced to elaborate further on its program than in the past. The party's ninety-three-page-long party program sheds significant light on what the Brotherhood's plans for a future Egypt look like, both in what the program explains and in which areas it chooses to remain ambiguous.[24]

The first clear aspect of the FJP program is the totality of its vision. There is no aspect of human life that the program does not aim to discuss and to put under state regulation. In what should seem bewildering to outside observers, the program leaves no detail unmentioned, from participation in cultural festivals abroad (pg. 85), to fast and free internet services (91), and even to publishing scholarly journals (33). While the Brotherhood has been criticized for years for its lack of a clear program, the view it takes of all human actions as regulated and supervised by the state leaves no room for doubt on the kind of state they aim to build. Looking more closely at the program's various sections helps explain this point.

The program starts by explaining what the FJP views as the intrinsic weaknesses of modern political parties, including their emphasis on and sole attention to practical matters such as legislation (4). Instead, the FJP program emphasizes other matters that are no less important than legislation and include the intellectual, spiritual, moral, and belief [*iman*] aspects of man. To prove the point, they quote the words of Christ: "Man shall not live by bread alone" (4). The program then explains that the goal of the party is "cleansing the soul and hearts, upgrading the feelings, refining the character, by calling for a commitment to worship, good manners, sociability and behavior, and to remind people of God, the Day of Judgment so as to wake up conscience" (4). The Mubarak regime had furthermore turned Egypt away from God and "into a colony of Western and Zionist policies." According to the program, "forgetting the Day of Judgment and God is one of the most important reasons that led to the Egyptian people's revolt" (5).

The program insists that the parliamentary system is the most suitable for Egypt (11).[25] And in an attempt to respond once and for all to the traditional Islamist criticism that true Muslims and activists should not involve themselves in parliamentary political life, the program answers by refusing to accept that politics is a dirty game and promises to tie politics to Islamic principles and values (6). The principles of Islamic Sharia are the main source of legislation (7), while the non-Muslim minority is given the right to resort to their own religious rulings in family and religious affairs (7).

As the FJP's program begins to describe in greater detail how every aspect of human activity should be regulated by the state, its major problems become clearer. In reforming the justice system, for instance, the program emphasizes reinstating the right of every citizen to raise a Hisbah case in court (14). Women "are entitled to all their rights," but only "if this is not inconsistent with the fundamental values of society and while achieving a balance between a women's duties and rights" (16). Civil society is encouraged and described as "a partner of the state in achieving the interests of society," but of course should not be permitted to operate against "the basic values of society" (17). Foreign policy naturally also gets its fair share in the document. Interference in the affairs of another state in the name of universal human rights is decried and so, too, is neo-liberalism and democracy promotion (21). "Arab and Islamic unity is one of the conditions of Egyptian national security" (22), and the Egyptian Israeli Peace Treaty is implicitly mentioned with the statement that treaties between states have to be accepted by the population (22). The "Zionist greed" in Sinai is explicitly addressed, and it is solved by state-led Muslim immigration to Sinai (22). Moreover, the Palestinian cause is described as "the most dangerous Egyptian national security case" because "the Zionist entity is an aggressive, expansionist, racist, and settler entity" (23).

On domestic issues, the FJP's program calls for many of the Islamist policies historically associated with the Brotherhood. The Brotherhood's historical obsession with the dangers posed to Egypt by foreign education is highlighted (29), and the program calls for Arabizing the teaching in universities (32), asserting that the goal of education is to "strengthen Arab and Islamic identity"(28). Scientific research is to be developed in order to "create a researcher that is committed to ethics and values" (32). Protecting the youth from "the cultural invasion that aims at weakening the nation" is very important (70), as "the cunning tricks of Western culture spoils and does not fix" (81). The role of houses of worship should be expanded to include a department combating illiteracy, committees for solving disputes, a department for educational services, and others (76). *Zakat* (charity) is to be collected by the government (76), and the national economy is to be based on the Islamic economic system (50).

While the program attempts to answer the worries of religious minorities and to reassure them, it also includes some proposals that are worrying for religious freedom. The document, for instance, includes an ambiguous statement that seems to indicate an attempt to bring the Christian endowments and the Church under state control (64). It also defines the future role of the Church as an institution that should work in "cooperation with different state institutions and Egyptian civil society to correct current deviant paths" (79).

The program is no less problematic concerning other social freedom. A new family law will be introduced based on Islamic Sharia (65), thus indicating the possible reversal of all gains made by Egyptian women in the realms of *khula* (divorce) and custody laws. Wives are granted the right to work "but without prejudice to the rights of the family and without prejudice to the provisions of Islamic Sharia" (65). On cultural matters, "the party adopts the view of the lack of separation between the moral and value system and the creative act" (81), and the document further states that, "the party emphasizes the importance of self-censorship of the Egyptian citizen" (82). The Egyptian cinema should of course "refrain from bad productions," (84) and it should operate with the FJP and civil society according to "a larger strategy of making the icon [or positive role models] in various areas of film, sports, the theater, literature, the press, and the media" (84). "Egyptian songs should be guided to a more ethical and creative horizon that is consistent with society's values and identity" (86). Moreover, the freedom of the press should also be limited to institutions "whose message corresponds to the values of society and public morals" (89).

Conclusion

THE UNPRECEDENTED FREEDOM THAT THE BROTHERHOOD ENJOYS AFTER THE REVolution has allowed it to maximize its benefits due to its highly effective organizational skills. While the new era brings enormous opportunities for the Brotherhood and could possibly lead to a complete Islamist take-over of the state, such an outcome is not a done deal. It will largely depend on how well the Brotherhood navigates through the different landmines that exist during this volatile transition period. Keeping a balance between appeasing the military to ensure their fast withdrawal from politics and strengthening an alliance with the non-Islamists could prove quite challenging. More challenging yet will be striking a similar balance between the Salafis and the non-Islamists. Furthermore, even if it manages all of these problems, the Brotherhood will still need to address the much larger and more difficult tasks of actually governing Egypt and living up to the high expectations and somewhat impossible hopes that Egyptians currently harbor.

The Brotherhood's long-term objective remains unchanged since its founding: the complete transformation of society along Islamic lines. In this regard, one of the movement's most potent weapons will likely be its infiltration of not only the civil service, which it has done for years, but also the military and police forces. The Brotherhood is insisting that its members can no longer be barred from joining these institutions. Since the revolution, it is virtually impossible to oppose such demands, as it would be ridiculous to allow a Brotherhood member to become prime minister yet reject him as a police or army officer. While today one may still speak of the military as an obstacle to the Brotherhood's quest for power, in a matter of years, this picture may be significantly changed. Analysts often argue that it is impossible for the Brotherhood to completely remake Egypt and that society would resist such attempts. True enough, but such optimism often downplays the transformative nature of totalitarianism.

NOTES

1. This tendency reached the absurd recently when the *New York Times* described Abdel Moneim Aboul Fetouh, a former MB member as a "Liberal Islamist." No explanation was given as to what the contradictory term meant. "A Long Peace is threatened in Israel Attack ." August 19, 2011. *New York Times.* Available at:

  http://www.nytimes.com/2011/08/20/world/middleeast/20egypt.html?ref=daviddkirkpatrick.

2. "MB's leader talks of God's role in Egyptian History." June 9, 2011. Ahram Online. Available at: http://english.ahram.org.eg/NewsContent/1/64/13985/Egypt/Politics-/MBs-leader-talks-of-Gods-role-in-Egyptian-history.aspx.

3. "MB chooses to Boycott second round of polls." December 1, 2010. Ikhwanweb. Available at: http://www.ikhwanweb.com/article.php?id=27387.

4. "Egyptian military court convicts 25 from Muslim Brotherhood, acquits 15." April 15, 2008. Voice of America. Available at: http://www.voanews.com/english/news/a-13-2008-04-15-voa43.html.

5. Brotherhood denies kidnapping candidate prior to runoffs." December 5, 2010. *The Daily News Egypt.* Available at: http://www.thedailynewsegypt.com/brotherhood-denies-kidnapping-candidate-prior-to-runoffs.html.

6. "Activists hope 25 January protest will be start of something big." January 24, 2011. Al Masry Al Youm. Available at: http://www.almasryalyoum.com/en/node/304368.

7. "Eisawey to Al Masry Al Youm: I will shoot those attempting to storm the Ministry of Interior." September 18, 2011. Al Masry Al Youm. Available at: http://www.almasryalyoum.com/node/496948.

8. "Muslim Brotherhood to start Dialogue with Egyptian government." February 6, 2011. Ria Novosti. Available at: http://en.rian.ru/world/20110206/162474411.html.

9. "Muslim Brotherhood says no objection to Suleiman as President." February 11, 2011. CNTV. Available at: http://english.cntv.cn/program/newshour/20110211/107025.shtml.

10. "Muslim Brotherhood says no Islamic Revolution in Egypt." February 5, 2011. *The Economic Times.* Available at: http://articles.economictimes.indiatimes.com/2011-02-05/news/28429392_1_muslim-brotherhood-vice-president-omar-suleiman-egyptian-people.

11. "Opposition Leader ElBaradei: Threat of Muslim Brotherhood is a myth lacking one iota of reality." January 30, 2011. Think Progress. Available at: http://thinkprogress.org/security/2011/01/30/141496/oppostion-leader-elbaradei-threat-of-muslim-brotherhood-is-a-myth-lacking-one-iota-of-reality/.

12. "Egypt Islamist Group denied political party license." September 20, 2011. Al Arabiya. Available at: http://english.alarabiya.net/articles/2011/09/20/167811.html.

13. "Historical leadership in Gama'a Islamia establish a new Party," September 23, 2011. Youm7. Available at: http://www.youm7.com/News.asp?NewsID=498413&SecID=12.

14. "Salafis protest to free Camilia Shehata." April 29, 2011. Youm7. Available at: http://english.youm7.com/News.asp?NewsID=339448.

15. "Jama'a al-Islamiya protests in front of US Embassy for release of Omar Abdel Rahman.' April 21, 2011. Al Masry Al Youm. Available at: http://www.almasryalyoum.com/en/node/408517.

16. Bargisi, Amr. "An Islamist President in Egypt?" September 12, 2011. *The Weekly Standard.* Available at: http://www.weeklystandard.com/articles/islamist-president-egypt_592143.html.

17. "Egypt Uprising: Islamists lead Tahrir Square rally." July 29, 2011. *BBC News*. Available at: http://www.bbc.co.uk/news/world-middle-east-14341089.

18. "Egypt political parties coalesce in readiness for parliamentary elections." September 13, 2011. Ahram Online. Available at: http://english.ahram.org.eg/NewsContent/1/64/20471/Egypt/Politics-/Egypt-political-parties-coalesce-in-readiness-for-.aspx.

19. "Egypt's oldest liberal party faces controversy over alliance with Brotherhood." September 7, 2011. Al Masry Al Youm. Available at: http://www.almasryalyoum.com/en/node/493401.

20. For a review of the different membership phases: Trager, Eric. "The Unbreakable Muslim Brotherhood," September/October 2011. *Foreign Affairs*. Available at: http://www.foreignaffairs.com/articles/68211/eric-trager/the-unbreakable-muslim-brotherhood.

21. "Badei: Aboul Fetouh violated his covenant with God." September 21, 2011. El Wafd. Available at: http://www.alwafd.org/%D8%A3%D8%AE%D8%A8%D8%A7%D8%B1%D9%88%D8%AA%D9%82%D8%A7%D8%B1%D9%8A%D8%B1/13/%D8%A7%D9%84%D8%B4%D8%A7%D8%B9%20%D8%A7%D9%84%D8%B3%D9%8A%D8%A7%D8%B3%D9%8A/98069/%D8%A8%D8%AF%D9%8A%D8%B9%D8%A3%D8%A8%D9%88%D8%A7%D9%84%D9%81%D8%AA%D9%88%D8%AD%D8%AE%D8%A7%D9%84%D9%81-%D8%B9%D9%87%D8%AF%D9%87-%D9%85%D8%B9-%D8%A7%D9%84%D9%84%D9%87.

22. "Former Brotherhood member tells group to stay out of politics." September 22, 2011. Bikya Masr. Available at: http://bikyamasr.com/43229/former-brotherhood-member-tells-group-to-stay-out-of-politics/.

23. Asked about who committed 9/11 Aboul Fetouh replied that: "I don't believe it was jihadists—it was too big an operation," he told me. "This was done by a country, not individuals. It's not a conspiracy theory—it's just logical. They didn't bring crimes before the U.S. justice system until now. Why? Because it's part of the conspiracy." Islam Lotfy, one of the "moderate" youth that analysts had placed hope in and who broke with the Brotherhood to form his own party answered, "I can't imagine someone flying for twenty minutes and nobody realizes it, and then another plane goes and crashes and then another in Pennsylvania," Trager, Eric. "Why is the Middle East still in thrall of 9/11 conspiracy theories?" September 3, 2011. *The New Republic*. Available at: http://www.tnr.com/article/world/94546/middle-east-radical-conspiracy-theories.

24. The detailed party program is available for download in Arabic on the FJP's official website: http://www.hurryh.com/. References will be to page numbers from this document.

25. The Parliamentary system with a weak President suits of course the Brotherhood quite well in the short term as they are not running for President.

The Spring of a New Political Salafism?

By Hassan Mneimneh

THE YEAR 2011 WILL UNDOUBTEDLY BE REMEMBERED AS PIVOTAL IN THE evolution of political thought and practice in the Arabic-speaking world. The revolutions, uprisings, and protests that have toppled regimes, and which are forcing many of the region's remaining autocrats to take defensive measures, have also transformed Arab political culture and the set of political choices previously available to ordinary Arabs.

Before the "Arab Spring," the prevailing assessment of political thought in the Arabic-speaking world identified Islamism as the main engine of political formulation and dissent. Secular and democratic ideas seemed weak by comparison, and the regimes themselves were suffering from systemic legitimacy crises that were due partly to the decline of nationalist ideologies. To the extent there was a contest of ideas, it was between competing currents of Islamism. Indeed, a multitude of Islamist streams appeared to dominate the political, intellectual, and cultural spheres. As a consequence of this, ordinary people were largely restricted to three courses of political action. First, they could accept autocratic rule and recognize its ability to bestow rewards and inflict punishments, either through passive acquiescence or direct complicity. Second, they could dissent by embracing one of the various currents of Islamism, which might favor a reformist or "accomodationist" approach to Islamic revival and political change, or it might lead to a more radical and rejectionist approach to the existing order. Third, people could succumb to the escapism offered by a popular culture constructed around unattainable notions of self-indulgence and consumerism.

In this pre-2011 configuration of Arab politics, democratic, liberal, progressive and secular ideas had seemingly no tangible influence, and they were implicitly rejected as irrelevant to Arab political realities by autocratic governments and the Islamist opposition alike. At the same time, both autocrats and Islamists acknowledged the existence and appeal of secular democratic principles insofar as this served their own agendas. Autocrats, for example, sought to fend off criticism from their Western partners over the restrictive political atmospheres they imposed by periodically making concessions to democratic demands—though they were always to keep the proponents of democracy marginal and ineffective. Islamists, too, acknowledged the existence of secular and liberal ideas in Arab societies—but only insofar as this offered proof of what the theocrats alleged was a Western onslaught of Islamic identity and values.

Thus far, however, the events of 2011 have demonstrated that both autocrats and theocrats had underestimated the appeal of secular and democratic ideas. Now, with the autocrats either out of power or on the defensive, the Islamists have been forced to respond openly to secular and democratic ideas and popular aspirations. This reality has prompted a reassessment of Islamist tactics and strategy.

Islamism in its multiple expressions remains a very potent force in Arab political culture today. Thanks to their substantial finance networks and organizational capacity, Islamists may even emerge as the immediate winners of the Arab Spring. However, Islamism no longer enjoys the virtually uncontested ideological supremacy that it once had on the Arab scene. Instead, the center of gravity of the political debate across the region has moved decisively away from the contest between autocrats and competing theocrats, and toward what only recently seemed to be the fringe. Now, the locus of the competition of ideas within Arab societies is between competing strains of Islamism and the positive propositions of secular democracy.

Importantly, this shift has occurred not because of intellectuals, but because of the success of activists in the field at mobilizing large crowds on the basis of concrete issues that resonate widely (in particular the injustices inflicted by the regimes, and the poor performances of some Arab economies). The shift was not produced nor has it been accompanied by a new, coherent secular democratic agenda or an intellectual deconstruction of the impasses of autocracy and theocracy. Nonetheless, the activists' success has created a new configuration in Arab political debate. The popular demands and slogans of the Arab Spring, which spread virally from one locale to the next, were simple: "*hurriyah, izzah, karamah*"—freedom, empowerment, dignity. While these demands were and remain poorly articulated, they were remarkable for the fact that they eschewed the ideas, concepts and values of Islamism.

The fact that the Arab Spring activists poured into the streets for something other than an "Islamic State" came as not only a surprise but a challenge to the Islamists—and especially to those who presumed to know and represent the aspirations of ordinary people. This has since become a central problem for Arab Islamist thought, as well as the subject of a new intra-Islamist debate. In fact, the Arab Spring has exposed a heretofore largely unsuspected weakness in Islamism. Unlike the activists of 2011, Islamists have not been as successful in recent years at mobilizing the Arab street in accordance with their ideological agenda. This is in part because Islamism in all its expressions is necessarily an elitist ideology, as it calls for a fundamental departure from aspects of Islam as it is *in actuality,* and also because it seeks to realize this departure through a program of "Islamization" led by a pious Islamist vanguard. As a reflection of this elitism, Islamist discourse is built on two patronizing conceits: one, that Muslim society and individuals are helplessly vulnerable to malevolent, non-Islamic influences and, two, that Muslims must be awoken from their "malaise" and "re-Islamized." In virtually all Islamist treatises, Muslim peoples are effectively immature and child-like, and can easily be swayed by Western plots and duped by crude Masonic-Zionist machinations.

Historically, an important source of disagreement among Islamists has been how to engage with the allegedly deficient people. Elements of the Muslim Brotherhood, for example, have advocated for a gradualist and "accomodationist" approach that tolerates a degree of non-Islamic ideas and practices in the interests of creating and maintaining a popular base for the movement. Various Salafist movements, meanwhile, have been far more ideologically rigid. As such, they have shown far less willingness to compromise with un-Islamic ideas and practices, and they have bluntly rejected any idea or course of action that is not properly rooted in Islam.

In this respect, Salafism generally may be considered more "elitist" than the reformist Islamism of the Brotherhood. This helps to account for some of the prestige and importance that has been associated with Salafism within the context of the larger Islamist universe. While the Salafist movement constitutes only a small minority within the Sunni branch of Islam, the disproportionate engagement with Salafist ideals by Islamists of all currents has helped to reinforce Salafism's own frequent claims to represent the "purest" and most "authentic" expression of Islamism. The Salafist movement, which is internally quite diverse, has in fact displayed more dynamism and ideological clarity than other streams of Islamism. In part because of Salafism's perceived religious purity relative to its Islamist rivals, and also because of the enormous oil funds available to the Salafist movement's worldwide outreach, Salafist ideology enjoyed an enormous influence on Arab political discourse before the Arab Spring.

Yet the swift falls of the regimes in Tunisia and Egypt and the continuing uprisings elsewhere have forced Islamists of all persuasions to alter their rhetoric and approach to the alleged immaturity and malaise of the people. Many Salafist currents have chosen to welcome and endorse the revolutions, while toning down their previously patronizing stance toward the people. Yet in the context of the Arab Spring, Salafism as a whole risks becoming irrelevant due to its ideological inflexibility and elitism. The Muslim Brotherhood, meanwhile, has sought to capitalize on the events by stressing the value and relevance of their gradualist approach to Islamization in the new Arab political context. Brotherhood activists now claim to fully embrace the popular slogans of the "Arab

Spring," and they contrast their position with the alienating elitism and rigidity of their Salafist rivals.

The popular uprisings of the Arab Spring have therefore put Islamist ideology as a whole, and Salafism in particular, to a test. Not only does Salafism face becoming increasingly irrelevant, but it also risks losing out to those Islamist rivals who may be better suited to adapt to the new configuration of Arab politics. As Salafist scholars and activists struggle to cope with the new political reality, it has already altered the internal constitution and ideology of their movement in dramatic ways.

The Emergence of Salafism

THE TERM "SALAFISM" (*al-salafiyyah*) IS A NEOLOGISM THAT REFERS TO A DYNAMIC SET of frequently divergent ideological currents that share common dogmatic foundations. If Islamism may be broadly understood as the ideological proposition that a radical understanding of Islam is relevant to or is to be assigned primacy in politics, then Salafism is eminently Islamist. However, contrary to Islamist movements like the Muslim Brotherhood that may tolerate or even seek an accommodation between an authentic "Islamic politics" and other forms of government, Salafism stipulates that political legitimacy resides exclusively in Islam as (Salafists believe) it was originally revealed. While Salafists broadly agree on this principle, they frequently disagree over the legitimacy and importance of political action in their overall effort to construct an Islamic State.

The Salafist movement began to cohere in its present form around a common set of precepts only in the past few decades. The promoters of Salafist ideology claim to represent the essence of Islam, as it was originally practiced by the Prophet Muhammad, his companions, and the early generations of Muslims. Referring to these early Muslims as *al-Salaf al-Salih*, or "the righteous predecessors," has been an accepted practice in Islamic scholasticism and jurisprudence for centuries. The use of derivatives from this designation to delineate a distinct set of political notions, however, is one product of the modern reform movement of the nineteenth century. The main intellectual architects of that movement, the Egyptian Azhari cleric Muhammad Abduh and his mentor Jamal al-Din al-Afghani, sought to demonstrate the compatibility of Islam with modernity. To accomplish this, they proposed a return to the original principles of the *al-Salaf al-Salih*, or to a "purified" Islam that was free of historical accretions and that, in their view, supported their progressive and modernizing vision. Their efforts have thus been characterized as *salafi-islahi*, or "reformist-purist."

To implement their project, Abduh and his disciples set out to identify and partner with a number of movements in the Islamic world that shared their agenda of religious reform and purity. However, the main criterion that they began with—the return to the pristine purity of the faith—allowed widely different interpretations, and thus proved too imprecise and fluid. This ultimately allowed for the inclusion of new ideas into the emerging *salafi-islahi* project that may have been consistent with the project's goals of religious reform and purity, but not its original modernizing vision. In the course of the early twentieth century, the emerging *salafi-islahi* movement thus began to intermix with the literalist teachings of Muhammad ibn 'Abd al-Wahhab of Arabia in the late eighteenth century, as well as the contemporary Sufi militant Sanusiyyah movement in North Africa. The incorporation of these and other ideas led to new debates and ultimately a split and divergence within the *salafi-islahi* intellectual trend between competing visions of reform and purity. By the 1920s and 1930s, both Hasan al-Banna (the founder of the Muslim Brotherhood and an early advocate of regimenting Muslims in a theocratic state) and Ali Abd al-Raziq (an Azhari scholar who sought to build a secular civil state rooted in Islamic doctrine) could legitimately claim to be the intellectual heirs to Muhammad Abduh's *salafi-islahi* project.

The decolonization and revolutions of the Arab world in the 1940s and 1950s produced a rapid evolution in Arab political thought, and the *salafi-islahi* project itself was supplanted by new political ideologies that sought legitimacy outside of an Islamic framework. Local versions of liberalism, nationalism, and socialism became the chosen ideologies of the elites that dominated Arab political discourse in the following decades. These elites accepted Islam as merely one element in the composition of the local and national identities. They also regarded religion as a declining force in society and politics.

The rise of Islamism in the latter part of the twentieth century has been due in no small part to the successive bankruptcies of these three grand political narratives and their failures to deliver on progress, "social justice," accountable governance, as well as a long-wished-for Arab victory over Israel. Moreover, at the dawn of the fifteenth Hijri century, four events took place and combined to establish the prominence of Islamism—and Salafism especially—in Arab political culture. The first of these events, the 1979 Islamic Revolution in Iran, demonstrated the possibility of overthrowing a repressive regime backed by the West. Second, the ultimately successful 1980 anti-Soviet Jihad in Afghanistan laid the operational infrastructure for a politically more potent Islamist and jihadist *internationale* that enjoyed great popular prestige. Third, the uprising of the Syrian branch of the Muslim Brotherhood against the al-Assad regime in Damascus, which ended with the 1982 Hama massacre, ultimately cemented Islamism's place as the primary anti-order ideology in the Arab world.

The spectacular fourth event—the takeover of the Meccan Holy Shrine by millenarian Islamists in 1979—may have been promptly contained and suppressed by the Saudi regime. The event, however, electrified Islamists everywhere, while serving as a catalyst for the further polarization of Arab politics. More fundamentally, the siege of Mecca was an expression of underlying developments within the religious doctrine and practice of Saudi Arabia that are still influencing Islamism, and the Muslim world more generally, to this day.

The Kingdom of Saudi Arabia, which was created through the conquests of Abd al-Aziz al-Saud in the 1920s, is the latest incarnation of the late eighteenth century partnership forged between the al-Saud tribe of Najd and the religious dynasty of al-Shaykh, who were heirs to the puritanical teachings of Muhammad ibn Abd al-Wahhab. The *dawa* of the latter deemed Sufi, Shiite and other Islamic doctrines as heretical, and called for their eradication. This ambition was given teeth by the military might of the latter, whose absolute temporal authority was, in exchange, confirmed by the religious authorities. With his kingship well-secured, Abd al-Aziz began to adjust the terms of the relationship between the monarchy and the religious authorities. The king eliminated the al-Ikhwan, the religious pan-tribal militia over which the clerical establishment had considerable influence, and compensated the religious scholars by granting them new authorities over the social life within his kingdom.

Abd al-Aziz's actions ultimately established the arrangements between the political and religious authorities of the Saudi kingdom that are still in place today. Moreover, by endowing the religious scholars with stability, influence, and an income (that grew geometrically with the advent of oil revenue), King Abd al-Aziz unwittingly enabled the religious institutions of Saudi Arabia to acquire a vastly disproportionate influence over Islamic thought globally. Nowadays, international students are invited to study at religious universities in Saudi Arabia so that they may serve once they return home as vectors for the propagation of Saudi-based religious ideas. Naturally, these students and their countries of origin are not passive recipients; the reception and use of Saudi ideas is conditioned by a multitude of factors, including their relevance and utility to other countries. Moreover, Saudi Arabian society is not immune to incoming influences either. Still, the availability of ideas incubated in Saudi Arabia as an option is made possible by the extraneous factor of oil wealth.

The many currents of modern Salafist ideology are themselves products of a still unfinished intermixing of and negotiation between ideas indigenous to Saudi society and foreign ideas, especially from Egypt. The doctrinal foundation of Salafism clearly derives from the austere and militant dawa of Muhammad ibn Abd al-Wahhab (who self-consciously followed the model of the thirteenth-century scholar ibn Taymiyyah). His successors in the Saudi Kingdom reinterpreted his teachings and institutionalized them by making them the ideology of an established clerical class funded by and supportive of the monarchy. The subsequent injection of political activism and the imperative of jihad that would come to challenge and counter the political quietism and unconditional loyalty to political authority that was once prevalent among Saudi religious scholars occurred through the popularization of the opinions of scholars from Egypt (such as Muhammad Qutb), Syria (such as Muhammad Surur Zayn al-Abidin), Palestine (such as Muhammad Azzam), and elsewhere.

Salafist Doctrine

THE SALAFIST MOVEMENT IN ITS MULTIPLE EXPRESSIONS IS BEST ANALYZED IN LIGHT of its scholastic dogma, socio-political agenda, and political ideology. The differences between Salafist currents are less pronounced at the level of the socio-political agenda (all seek a return to an "Islamic State") and are minor to non-existing at the basic level of scholastic dogma. The distinctions between Salafist currents arise largely as a consequence of their different tactics and political ideologies, which nowadays range from requiring an unqualified obedience to the will of the ruler to mandating Islamic insurgency.

The scholastic approach of Salafism consists of the reliance on the Quran and the Sunnah of the Prophet, as understood by his companions and the righteous among his early followers. The basic tenets of this approach are strict monotheism (*tawhid*), total obedience to the commandments of the Prophet (*taah*), and a continuous effort to purify one's thoughts and actions in conformity with the sayings and deeds of the Prophet (*tazkiyat al-nafs*). Salafism's proponents routinely insist that they adhere to a methodological approach (*manhaj*) and not a school of jurisprudence (*madhhab*). They also insist that the Salafist method is compatible with all the established schools of jurisprudence of Sunni Islam. This self-definition of Salafism is deliberately meant to appear non-polemical, although Salafists normally supplement it with a number of qualifications that reveal their intrinsic ideological hostility toward other Islamic schools.

Customarily, the identification of the religious credentials of engaged and learned Sunni Muslims required the indication of an individual's affinity with schools and/or currents in three complementary aspects of religious life: theology (*aqidah*), jurispridence (*madhhab fiqhi*), and ritualistic practice (*tariqah*). Among Sunnis, the dominant theological school is the Ashari school, and the minority Maturidi and Athari schools compete for a distant second. There are four recognized schools of Sunni jurisprudence: the Maliki school, which is spread across North and Sub-Saharan Africa; the Shafii school that prevails in Egypt, much of the Levant, the Hijaz, Yemen, and parts of Asia; the Hanafi school, which dominates in parts of the Levant and Iraq, Turkey, and large swaths of Central and South Asia; and the Hanbali school, which is entrenched in the Najd area of Arabia. Far more variety historically exists (and still does, albeit decreasingly) at the ritualistic practice level, with the Qadiri, Naqshbandi, Rifai, Shadhili, Tijani, Ahmadi, and many others constituting unique families of ritualistic approaches that are steeped in the mystical wealth of Sufism. The available options in all three aspects of religious life were traditionally understood as mutually compatible (although certain combinations were more common than others). It is thus possible for a learned Muslim to be Hanafi in matters of jurisprudence, Maturidi or Ashari in theology, and Naqshbandi or Qadiri or Rifai in ritualistic practice, and so forth.

While Salafism's claim to be a methodology is simple and seemingly non-polemical, it seeks in practice the deconstruction of virtually the totality of this conventional system of Islamic identification. For example, Salafism deems ritualistic practice at best as a forbidden innovation (*bidah*), and rejects *in toto* all of its local expressions. While both the Ashari and Maturidi schools of theology seek a harmonization of reason and revelation, Salafism rejects both schools as contaminated by non-Islamic philosophical ideas, heterodox, or even heretic. The only theological school that Salafism accepts as valid is the literalist Athari school. (In actual fact, even though Salafists routinely claim the opposite, traditional Athari and modern Salafi theologies both engage in considerable *kalam* constructions—*kalam* being the dynamic Islamic theological-philosophical discipline that was originally built on Hellenic and Hellenistic foundations. Ibn Taymiyyah's reconceptualization of pure monotheism as a recognition of both the Lordship (*rububiyyah*) and Divinity (*uluhiyyah*) of God—a conceptualization that is at the core of the Salafist dogma—is in language and structure a continuation of the exercise of *kalam*. In matters of jurisprudence, Salafists trace their methodological approach to *ahl al-hadith*, a scholastic teaching from early Islamic history that utilized only certain Prophetic traditions (*hadith*) with trustworthy chains of transmission to determine authoritative norms for social and political behavior. This scholastic approach differs greatly from the rule-based exercise of jurisprudence that was developed by the *ahl al-rai* school and greatly influenced the historical development of Islamic jurisprudence. As such, Salafism places itself at odds with the dominant currents of jurisprudence in three of the four major schools of jurisprudence. Only the Hanbali school of jurisprudence, which has the smallest original global footprint, is spared substantive criticism from Salafism.

In fact, Salafists commonly praise Ahmad ibn Hanbal, the founder of the Hanbali school of jurisprudence and source of the Athari school of theology, as an archetypal Salafist. Because of this, Salafists may be assumed to be merely a modern Hanbali faction. However, in line with the arguments of the fifteenth-century religious scholar and activist Ahmad ibn Taymiyyah, whom they credit with the "revival" of their methodological approach, Salafists (nominally) de-emphasize the importance of schools of jurisprudence, while insisting on the need for methodological rigor in pursuit of their identified priorities.

While the Salafist movement may resist the exclusive identification of their ideology with Hanbali jurisprudence—(indeed, scholars from other traditions have also declared themselves "Salafists" in their approach)—the Hanbali and, specifically, the Najdi roots of the movement are clearly evident in Salafist political ideology. While the Najd region of Arabia historically shared with the rest of the Muslim world the quasi-exclusive dominance of the dynastic model of political leadership, the socio-economic realities of this remote desert province meant that it neither developed its primitive governance institutions nor attracted to it conquest by more developed states. While in other settings the

Islamic scholastic tradition routinely interacted with, influenced, and accepted evolving political systems, the Najdi dawa had no comparable exposure, and thus treated all such systems as forbidden innovation. This Najdi dawa is evident today in the dismissive way Salafists speak about and reject the political institutions with which learned and devout Muslims outside of Najd have historically interacted. It also helps to explain some of the major inconsistencies between Salafist religious and political discourse. On the one hand, Salafism presents itself as a revival of the original practice of the faith rightly understood. On the other hand, Salafist political practice shows its Najdi roots and biases through its acceptance of kingship and dynastic rule and its vocal rejections of all political institutions and ideas that seem to depart from these Najdi norms. This is despite the fact that explicit verses in the Quran reject kingship (Quran, 27:34), and also despite the fact that dynastic rule was not the practice of *al-Salaf al-Salih*.

Despite their claims to the contrary, Islamism in general and Salafism in particular do not offer a political counter-model for the modern political systems that they reject. The multitude of texts they invoke from the classical Islamic tradition discuss and debate the personal qualities of the just ruler, and they also offer rulers advice on virtuous conduct. Yet, these texts do not offer a basis for political theory. In fact, the central claims of Islamism—that Islam is a "total system," and that the "political" in Islam cannot be dissociated from the "religious"—are themselves modern constructs that have gained credence and legitimacy largely because of the absence of any political theory in the Islamic scholastic traditions that might form the basis for a counter-argument. One of Islamism's greatest paradoxes resides in its unwillingness to concede the verifiable fact that it is a modern construction coupled with its inability to develop new models on the basis of Islamic principles. The latter aspect is largely due to the restrictions that Salafism, with its essentially Najdi political outlook, has managed to impose on itself and the rest of Islamism in the course of its ascendancy over the last several decades. Moreover, since its frame of reference is explicitly limited to the duration of the message of the Prophet Muhammad (twenty-two years in mid-sixth century AD), and since it strictly applies the "no innovation" rule, Salafist ideology has become a serious impediment to the Islamist exploration of new ideas and approaches. The methodological rigor promoted by the scholastic dogma of Salafism has therefore worked not only to dismantle the Islamic religious system, but it has also affected social and political life across the Islamic world.

Evolution and Gradation

SOME DIFFERENCES AMONG SALAFISTS ON ELEMENTS OF DOGMA HAVE GIVEN RISE TO countless debates within and among different Salafist streams of thought. One issue that has caused enormous controversy is the revived notion of *irja*, which calls for the suspension of the denunciation of perceived transgressions against the Divine commandments of rite. This notion was espoused by an early Islamic school known as "the Murjiah," who considered judgment over such transgressions to fall exclusively within God's jurisdiction. No pronouncement or action was therefore expected from Muslims if a fellow Muslim were to disobey ritualistic and/or belief commandments. The early opponents of the Murjiah considered their teachings to be a license for apostasy, and the school did not survive for long as an Islamic denomination. They are instead treated by the mainstream Islamic tradition as but one example among many of heterodoxy within early Islam; in their particular case, the Murjiah are accused of the "excess" of not safeguarding the religion against dissolution.

Modern Salafism espouses and amplifies the Islamic injunction to promote good actions and denounce bad deeds. To most Muslims, this injunction is generally understood as a call for individuals to proactively engage society; in modern Saudi Arabia, the injunction has also become the Salafist justification for the religious police (*hayat al-amr bi-l-maruf wa-l-nahi an al-munkar*). Yet the Saudi religious police, as invasive as it is, is practically incapable of enforcing Islam and policing actions that take place in the home, or in a foreign country. The Salafist pronouncements on such out-of-sight actions have oscillated between condemnation and suspension of judgment, with accusations of *irja* facing the proponents of the latter view. The mutual accusations of *irja* by one scholar against another have thus become an effective engine for enhancing the overall rigidity of Salafist doctrine and sharpening the differences between opposing Salafist currents. (The counter-accusations to *irja*—*ghulw* (exaggeration) and *takfir* (denunciation as apostasy)—have not acquired the negative connotation of *irja,* and thus have not yet commanded the vigorous self-defense and further hardening of different positions within Salafism that the accusation of *irja* generates.)

Such polemics notwithstanding, Salafism's multiple currents generally do share a common foundation in dogma; the differences between them, where they exist, are often due to differences in political tactics and ideology. On the eve of the Arab revolutions in 2011, one of the most important areas of gradation among the multiple Salafist currents was their respective positions on the Islamic legitimacy of political activism, which was originally a notion imported into Salafism from other Islamist movements, in particular the Muslim Brotherhood. These different positions on the religious legitimacy of political activism has been reflected in the Salafist movement's mixed responses to the Arab Spring and in the new trajectories of Salafism's diverse currents over the last year.

Scholastic Salafism, sometimes identified as *al-salafiyyah al-ilmiyyah* (though this designation is sharply contested), is explicitly apolitical, and avoids whenever possible any pronouncement on political issues. Scholars within this current ordinarily focus on matters of jurisprudence and theology; on the basis of the ongoing study of Prophetic traditions, they routinely enunciate on prescribed and proscribed behavior in religious and transactional practices (*ibadat* and *muamalat*), and on what distinguishes sound belief from apostasy.

The Saudi Wahhabi religious establishment is the primary locus of this particular Salafist current, although its influence is not restricted to Saudi Arabia. (Indeed, the most prominent and prolific practitioner of Scholastic Salafism in the past decades has been Muhammad Nasir al-Din al-Albani (d. 1999), a Syrian resident of Jordan, of Albanian origin.) Scholastic Salafists in Saudi Arabia regularly produce fatwas at the request of the monarchy, and thus lend religious authority to the monarchy's official positions. The wording of these fatwas, however, often only narrowly serve the purpose intended, and they often leave much open to interpretations. For this among other reasons, Scholastic Salafism is often accused of a lack of coherence.

In response to the uprising in Bahrain in February 2011, the Saudi Council of Senior Scholars (*hayat kibar al-ulama*), which is the most prominent institution of Scholastic Salafism, issued a fatwa forbidding demonstrations against an established ruler. However, the positions of members of the council with respect to the uprising in Syria in the subsequent months was considerably different. Two prominent council members, Salih al-Luhaydan[1] and Salih al-Fawzan, vociferously attacked the Syrian regime and expressed their support for the protestors.

While the two scholars' positions toward the uprisings in Bahrain and Syria reflect those of the Saudi government, the scholars "protected" themselves against accusations of being "political" by providing a religious justification for their stand, rather than a political one. They were careful, for example, in their support for the Syrian revolution to refer to the anti-Islamic character of the Assad regime, which is based on a secularist ideology, and led by a president whose religious affiliation (Alawite) is heretical in the judgment of Salafism.

In the past, such juristic acrobatics, combined with Scholastic Salafism's economy of words on controversial issues and the political quietism of the current's main figures (such as Abd al-Aziz ibn Baz (d. 1999), Muhammad ibn Salih al-Uthaymin (d. 2001), and Abd Allah ibn Abd al-Rahman al-Jibrin (d. 2009)), has led some Islamist activists to denounce Scholastic Salafists as the "ruler's scholars" (*ulama al-sultan*). At the same time, Scholastic Salafism's ambiguity on politics has also been interpreted by some of its adherents as lending tacit approval to radical action. This ambiguity has protected Scholastic Salafism as a common denominator, at a somehow equal distance from at least two other currents of Salafism. Both activist and loyalist Salafists (as described below) could thus portray themselves as consistent with the core mandated by Scholastic Salafism. This ambiguity is likely to continue to be the *modus operandi* of Scholastic Salafism amidst the ongoing political transformations of the Arab world.

Activist Salafism, or *al-salafiyyah al-daawiyyah*, borrows its focus on social engagement from activist forms of Islamism like the Muslim Brotherhood, while remaining within the doctrinal confines of Salafism. Although this current's main emphasis is on social and cultural affairs, elements of political ideology and behavior are evident in pronouncements and create potential for mobilization.

Activist Salafism emerged as a reaction to the sclerotic inability of Scholastic Salafism to confront and respond to Western ideologies in general (liberal, socialist, secularist), and in particular to attempts by Muslim reformers to recast these ideologies in a Muslim garb (such as the projects of Nasr Hamid Abu Zayd, Muhammad Arkun, and Hasan Hanafi to understand Islamic revelation in historical, humanistic, or materialistic terms).[2] The emergence of this current of Salafism in Saudi Arabia in conjunction with the Awakening Movement (*al-sahwah*) of the 1980s injected pride and polemics into the cultural sphere, and promoted a remedial degree of tolerance and flexibility in the social and religious practice realms. It also introduced a new generation of public intellectuals, including most notably Safar al-Hawali, Salman al-Awdah, Aid al-Qarni, and Nasir al-Umar.

Activist Salafism introduced Saudi society to the novel notion of a "loyal opposition," as some of this current's leading figures publicly engaged in a (tame) criticism of the Saudi Monarchy. As a result of this dissent, many Activist Salafists spent extended stays in jail. They later turned to self-criticism as they retreated to a more assertive loyalism in reaction to the intensifying agitations against the monarchy of their jihadist counterparts. Activist Salafists are also often accused by their critics of "internationalism" for raising in the public sphere concerns beyond the local.

Activist Salafism's support for the uprisings in the Arab world has been vocal, even when the official Saudi stance towards these movements has been skeptical or negative.[3] Indeed, Activist Salafism appears to be widening the scope of its borrowing from other Islamist movements. In fact, while the Muslim Brotherhood, which is in actuality an umbrella of heterogeneous currents, seems to be undergoing a degree of internal fragmentation, a convergence can be noted in the range of movements that separated it from Salafism. In their anticipation of a gradualist Islamist appropriation of the Arab Spring, the differences between Activist Salafists, the more orthodox members of the Muslim Brotherhood, Tahriris, and Sururis, are narrowing.[4]

Loyalist Salafism was once self-identified as "*salafiyya ahl al-wala*,"[5] but today it is more commonly referred to by the quasi-pejorative designation of "al-Jamiyyah," or the followers of Muhammad Aman al-Jami (d. 1994). This current rejects any form of activism, whether social or political, as an infringement on the prerogatives of the ruler (*wali al-amr*). It places an unconditional trust in the established Muslim ruler at the forefront of the understanding of religious obligations—even if the nominally Muslim ruler transgresses religious commandments.

In the aftermath of the fall of Baghdad to U.S. and coalition troops in 2003, the adherents to Loyalist Salafist teachings in Iraq[6] claimed that Muslims were obligated to obey non-Muslim rulers if their rule is imposed by force. In Saudi Arabia, this current emerged as a reaction to the Awakening Movement, whose "loyal opposition" to the monarchy was seen by Loyalist Salafists as a charade in preparation for an overall insurgency and takeover. The most prominent scholar of this current in Saudi Arabia is Rabi al-Madkhali (and hence this Salafist strain is sometimes referred to as al-Madkhaliyyah).

Contrary to Scholastic Salafists who (generally) restrict their pronouncements to opinions on issues of theology and jurisprudence, Loyalist Salafist scholars often engage in the discipline of *al-jarh wa-l-tadil*, or the critical assessment of individuals. As a result, a great deal of the scholarly energies of Loyalist Salafists are devoted to polemics, apologetics, and intra-Salafist feuds.

Loyalist Salafists have assumed an openly negative position toward the uprisings in the Arab world. On the eve of the January 25th demonstration that marked the beginning of the Egyptian revolution, the prominent "Salafist Association" (*al-jama ahl al-salafiyyah*) in Alexandria issued a statement declaring that the consensus among its scholars was to reject the demonstrations as non-conforming with religious commandments.[7] Later, in an effort to undermine the uprising in Libya, Muammar Qaddafi's regime used automated phone calls to broadcast a recording of Rabi al-Madkhali that denounced the Arab protests as acts of sedition and commanded followers to join forces with established leaders.[8] Today, Loyalist Salafism finds itself in the midst of the Arab Spring discredited and on the defensive. Its doctrinal rigidity, however, does not permit it to readily adjust itself to the new realities; for this reason, Loyalist Salafism appears poised to wane in influence.

Jihadist Salafism, or *al-salafiyyah al-jihadiyyah*, represents a minority Salafist faction, but it has nonetheless commanded considerable support and respect in many Islamist circles. Jihadist Salafism teaches that the will of established political rulers may and should be bypassed in order to fulfill the injunction of jihad, or religiously-mandated war. The injunction of jihad is understood by Jihadi Salafi preachers as applicable and obligatory on all individuals. This contrasts with the prevailing scholastic understanding of the injunction of jihad, which holds that the conditions of its applicability ought to be determined solely by the ruler, and that the obligation to undertake jihad is incumbent on the state, not the individual.

When Jihadist Salafism first emerged in Saudi Arabia it was seen as a departure from the Salafist norms, although it was tolerated as long as its context was amorphous. Meanwhile, the romantic image of the jihadist rebel—a man who questioned political authority and followed higher principles, while traveling abroad in defense of victimized fellow Muslims—gained considerable allure, despite the death and mayhem that jihadist networks began to afflict on their targets in the 1980s. By 2005, however, the Jihadist Salafist insurgency was displaying its deeds and values in Saudi Arabia itself, with gruesome killings and wanton destruction. The moral credit of Jihadist Salafism within Saudi society has since been depleted.

The killing by U.S. Special Forces in May 2011 of Osama bin Laden, who was portrayed in some Salafist narratives as selfless, stoic, and heroic (though perhaps also a bit misguided), further dissipated Jihadist Salafism's "moral credit" and prestige. The death of bin Laden has also left the jihadist movement exposed to the substantive failure that the popular uprisings of the Arab Spring have revealed. Three decades since the onset of the anti-Soviet Afghan Jihad and the emergence of a Jihadist *Internationale*, more than two decades after the Saudi monarchy had sought Western protection, against the loud objections of the Jihadists, and almost a decade after the jihadist "raids" of September 11, 2001, meant to ignite the millennial confrontation with the usurpers of the rights of the *ummah*, Jihadist mobilization in Arab and Muslim societies has still not managed to ignite a revolution.

What the transformations in the Arab world, unfolding in 2011, demonstrate is that the failure of the mobilization is not due to deficiency in the base, but in the message. In fact, the Arab protesters were not motivated by Islamist or jihadist slogans, but by values and aspirations alien to Jihadist Salafism. The realization that Jihadist Salafism needs to reinvent itself to survive is evident in the discourse of the current's ideologues.[9] The movement's survival in the era of the Arab Spring, however, will likely depend more on its ability to thwart the emergence of alternative means of expression in the Arab world than on any self-reinvention.

Above Activist, Below Jihadist

THE PRESENTLY IDENTIFIABLE TRAJECTORIES WITHIN THE DIFFERENT CURRENTS OF Salafism point to a larger tendency within activist Salafism to allow for political action. This movement will likely lead to a deepening of divisions and a potential fracture within the Activist Salafist stream, with a segment of this current remaining loyal to the Salafist refusal to recognize any political system outside of the imagined Islamic state, and another faction resorting to arguments based on the Islamic principle of demonstrable interest (*maslahah*) to justify its pragmatic engagement in politics.

The self-organization of many Egyptian Salafists into the Al Nour political party is illustrative both of this break within Activist Salafism, as well as of a new process of convergence between some Political Salafists and orthodox elements of the Muslim Brotherhood. Al Nour accepts the electoral system, softens the entrenched Salafist rhetoric toward non-Muslims, and pledges gradualism in pursuit of its declared goals of "reconstructing" society along Islamic norms.[10]

While the Salafists who have joined Al Nour explicitly proclaim their intent to forge alliances with other Islamists, the Salafist activists and the movement as a whole has been blamed for much of the communal violence in post-revolutionary Egypt, which has included deadly attacks on Coptic churches and Sufi shrines. To intransigent jihadists, such sectarian violence may prove the best way to remain relevant and improve their declining fortunes after the Arab Spring. However, not all Salafists appear willing to embrace this agenda. Indeed, some Salafists have protested, claiming they are not to blame.[11] They have also complained Salafism has a negative image in Egypt, and have tried to persuade others that the communal violence has been committed by remnants of the previous regime.[12]

Whether the issue is to contain jihadist splinter groups or to maintain their public image, Salafism in Egypt and elsewhere after the Arab Spring can no longer afford to remain politically quietist. With the discrediting and decline of jihadism relative to other Islamist ideologies, and the success of a popular revolution based on peaceful protest, the course of action available to Salafists in Egypt and elsewhere who wish to remain relevant in the era of the Arab Spring is "above social activism, below jihadism." For this to be achieved, a reassessment of Salafist approaches, if not dogma, remains in order, and will likely be the focus of the movement in the time ahead.

NOTES

1. For the anti-Asad Assad fatwa of of Salih al-Luhaydan see http://www.youtube.com/watch?v=DrphhE-qgpEM. For Salih al-Fawzan's Fawzan's comments on the uprising in Syria, see http://www.youtube.com/watch?v=zIrOtvSXww4.

2. For a first-person description of the intellectual environment that prompted the emergence of the Sahwah, see http://www.aawsat.com/details.asp?section=17&article=232184&issueno=9290, an interview with Jamal Sultan, a prominent figure in the launch of the movement.

3. For Salman al-Awdah's support for the Egyptian revolution, see http://amoaagsherif.ahlamontada.com/t6767-topic; http://www.albarbhary.net/vb/showthread.php?t=1757 chronicles the polemics between activist and loyalist Salafism on the issue of protests.

4. While the Muslim Brotherhood constitutes the flagship of (non-Salafist) Islamist political activism, two of its off-shoots complete the triad of dominant approaches; the Tahriris (of Hizb al-Tahrir) qualify the MB approach with less focus on mass mobilization and more on institutional penetration, while the Sururis (followers of Muhammad Sururu Zayn al-Abidin) insist on more doctrinal conformity. The MB, Tahriris, and Sururis, have constituted a magnet for Salafists who desire more activism. One example stressing the need for a more dynamic approach to jurisprudence in Salafism, along lines similar to their Islamist rivals, is http://majles.alukah.net/showthread.php?t=82228.

5. For the circumstances surrounding the abandonment of this designation, and their retreat to the generic Salafist one, see Abu Qutadah al-Falastini, "Bayna manhajayn" (Between Two Approaches) http://www.tawhed.ws/pr?i=858.

6. *Dahr al-muthallib li-jawaz tawliyat al-muslim ala muslim min kafirin mutaghallib* (The refutation of the criticism on the permissibility of appointment of Muslims to rule upon Muslims by forceful non-Muslims), a compilation of historical opinions and edicts, printed and distributed in Iraq in 2004. For a Loyalist Salafist endorsement of the book, see http://www.albaidha.net/vb/showthread.php?t=18717.

7. http://gate.ahram.org.eg/News/35329.aspx.

8. http://www.muslm.net/vb/showthread.php?t=424750. Considerable confusion persists as to whether al-Madkhali himself has authorized such use.

9. For an illustrative example of a jihadist ideologue's self-criticism, see http://www.muslm.net/vb/showthread.php?t=424817.

10. http://www.alnourparty.org/page/program_headers.

11. http://www.ahram.org.eg/Investigations/News/77060.aspx.

12. An example of a Salafist self-assessment of potential futures is provided at http://majles.alukah.net/showthread.php?t=14556.

Islam in the National Story of Pakistan

By Aparna Pande

PAKISTAN WAS NOT ORIGINALLY IMAGINED AS AN ISLAMIC STATE. AND YET TODAY, according to a 2009 report by the British Council, more than seventy-five percent of Pakistanis consider themselves to be Muslims first and Pakistani nationals second.[1] Moreover, a May 2011 survey by the Gilani Research Foundation, a Pakistan-based polling organization, showed that sixty-seven percent of Pakistanis favored state-led Islamization of their country.[2] How could this have happened in a country that was founded only a few generations ago by a secular, Westernized elite as the homeland for South Asia's Muslims?

The political turmoil and growing radicalization of Pakistani society have their roots in an ideologically-driven Islamic Pakistani identity. The Islamist narrative on which the country's identity and politics are based has been constructed and crafted in such a way that even secular Muslims have inadvertently contributed to both its rise and spread in Pakistan. The roots of this narrative lie in the political beliefs that emerged among wealthy Muslims of British India in the late nineteenth century.

EVER SINCE ISLAM WAS FIRST INTRODUCED ON THE INDIAN SUBCONTINENT IN the tenth century and up to the early modern era, South Asia's Muslims did not consider themselves to be a minority population living amongst India's Hindu majority. Instead, they understood themselves to be the rightful rulers of the subcontinent, as well as politically and culturally superior to their counterparts. However, with the advent of British colonial rule and the gradual introduction of parliamentary democracy, Indian Muslims became increasingly aware of their status as a numerical minority—and also of Islam's declining political and cultural power. In the age of parliamentary democracy, numbers mattered far more than in the era of Muslim monarchs.

The establishment of British rule and the subsequent rise of Hindu power produced two broad strands of nationalism among Indian Muslims. To some Muslim leaders, nationalism was primarily understood in territorial terms: India's Muslims may adhere to a different religion than the Hindus of India, but both populations belonged to a common Indian homeland and nationality. These leaders by and large joined the Indian National Congress, a secular nationalist party formed in 1885 that included a small percentage of Muslims in its leadership. Meanwhile, other Muslim leaders maintained that religion, rather than territory, was the defining characteristic of identity and nationalism. In their view, Hindus and Muslims were not merely followers of different religions but members of two different communities or nations. This belief formed the crux of the so-called "two-nation theory," which in later years was used by Muslim leaders to justify the creation of the state of Pakistan as an independent Muslim homeland that was separate from "Hindu India."

During the Raj period, the majority of Indian Muslim leaders were modern and western-educated Muslims who were not part of the traditional, Mughal-era religious establishment. Nonetheless, many of these modern elites considered Islam to be the defining aspect of their identity. Sir Sayyid Ahmed Khan, a leading reformer and the intellectual founder of the Muslim Anglo-Oriental College at Aligarh (which was later renamed Aligarh Muslim University), was among those who believed Muslims, as a religious and political minority, could only find safety on the subcontinent if they allied with the British and distanced themselves politically from the Hindus. Paradoxically, Sir Sayyid Ahmed Khan also had many close Hindu friends, and he was known to have described Hindus and Muslims as "the two beautiful eyes" of a common India.

Subsequent generations of Muslim leaders also held similarly conflicting views concerning Muslim identity and nationalism within the context of India. For example, Indian Muslim leaders like Pakistan's founding father, Muhammad Ali Jinnah, had many close Hindu and Parsee (Zoroastrian) friends. Yet he espoused the "two-nation theory," and called for the strict separation of religious communities for political reasons. Later, after Pakistan achieved independence in 1947, the country's secular leaders saw no contradiction between accepting a nationalist identity rooted in religion and maintaining their secular credentials.

A deep-seated distrust of Hindus and a strong desire for guarantees that Muslims would have a meaningful voice in Indian politics led the Indian Muslim elite to champion the idea of creating separate electorates for Muslims and Hindus. Throughout British India, the implementation of parliamentary democracy led to the creation of a number of territory-based constituencies that in turn elected representatives to the legislative assemblies. In a Hindu-majority country, however, Muslim leaders had to face the reality that a common parliamentary electoral system invariably meant that the majority of parliamentarians would be Hindu. To have a meaningful say in any future government,

Muslims therefore needed to ensure that a certain minimum number of Muslim representatives were elected. They could achieve this objective either by ensuring that all political parties had a certain number of Muslim candidates (which would effectively use the minority bloc's voting clout) or they could ask for separate, community-based electorates.

In 1905, a delegation of the Muslim leaders, led by the Aga Khan, went to meet the Viceroy in Simla, Lord Minto, to ask for the provision of separate electorates. Although the inclusion of this provision in the 1909 Minto-Morley Reforms was viewed by many members of the Muslim elite as a positive step, it was alternatively seen by the Indian National Congress as a "divisive" British ploy meant to cripple an emerging Indian national identity. At first, the right to vote was very limited, and so the institution of separate voting didn't affect day to day politics for ordinary people. However, among the elites who could vote, the adoption of the system of separate electorates ultimately helped cement a deep sense of political separation between the religious communities.

The establishment in 1906 of the All India Muslim League at Dacca, in modern day Bangladesh, represented one manifestation of the growing belief that Muslims needed their own organizations, separate from Hindu-led organizations, to represent them and help safeguard their community interests. The Muslim League were staunch advocates of separate electorates and of reserving seats for Muslims in the legislative assemblies of Muslim-minority provinces, and they also demanded that the league be involved directly in any discussion about the future of India. It was on these grounds that the Muslim League competed in the first provincial-level parliamentary elections in British India in 1936. By championing these causes, the Muslim League's leaders believed that they could win enough parliamentary seats to establish the league as the "Sole Spokesman" of all of the Muslims in British India, according to the historian Ayesha Jalal.[3]

The Muslim League was ultimately defeated in the 1936 elections, but the elections marked a major turning point in the quest for a separate homeland for India's Muslims. The setback led the Muslim League to change its overall policy from simply asking for political guarantees for minority representation to demanding equal status as a separate nation. The loss caused it to pursue the goals of political separation and autonomy with new focus and vigor. Instead of pressing for safeguards for the Muslim minority, the league began to demand the formal implementation of the two-nation theory, asserting that Hindus and Muslims, despite their numerical differences, possessed an equal right to decide the future of India.

In the context of the 1946 elections, which would decide who would rule the Indian subcontinent after the British, the league's leadership felt that it was more important than ever to establish the league as the sole Muslim voice and party in the Raj. Due to the enormous cultural, ethnic, and linguistic differences among the Muslim populations living in the various provinces of British India, the league's campaign strategy to win support emphasized the separateness of the Muslim and Hindu nations. The free use of Islamic slogans and symbols thus became a common feature of the 1946 elections. In one campaign speech, Muhammad Ali Jinnah, then the president of the All India Muslim League, declared to Muslims, "if you want Pakistan, vote for the League candidates," and he further warned that if Muslims failed to "realize [their] duty today" they would be "reduced to the status of *Sudras* (or low caste Hindus) and Islam [would] be vanquished from India."[4] To win the support of India's diverse Muslim communities, the Muslim League additionally sought help from and forged alliances with more traditional Islamic social and political institutions, including landowners (*zamindars*), clan- and community-based (*biraderi*) networks, and the hereditary religious elites (*pirs/sajjadanashins*).

While the "two-nation theory" proved useful as a tool for mobilization in India before its partition, the starkly different politics of modern Pakistan and India clearly show that religion is an unreliable basis for national identity. In the new state of India, leaders of the Congress like Jawaharlal Nehru (a secular socialist), Sardar Vallabhai Patel (a conservative Hindu nationalist), and Maulana Abul Kalam Azad (a conservative Muslim nationalist) all held a territorially-defined, rather than religiously-based, view of nationalism. This helped to bind the religiously and ethnically diverse provinces of India together, and India's political leaders were thus able to address the vitally important practical tasks of writing a new constitution and implementing their economic, security, and foreign policy agendas.

In Pakistan, however, the Muslim League's political use of religion as the basis for a separate Islamic state gave rise to a central question that has bedeviled Pakistan ever since its creation: "If Islam is to be the basis of the state, whose Islam will be followed and how?" When Pakistan was created, the majority of its leaders were relatively secular and politically moderate men like Mr. Jinnah and Mr. Liaquat Ali Khan. However, once religion was incorporated as an essential component of national ideology, it became impossible to remove it from the political life of the new nation. Consequently, the crafting of a Pakistani national identity required the use of Islam and routine appeals to Muslim distinctiveness, and this has haunted Pakistan's political life ever since.

I N 1949, PAKISTAN'S CONSTITUENT ASSEMBLY APPROVED *The Objectives Resolution of Pakistan*, which articulated the goals of the new state and the guiding principles of the future national constitution. In some ways it was ironic that the new state's objectives were not decided and announced until two years after the actual formation of Pakistan. *The Objectives Resolution* effectively attached the identity of the Pakistani state to Islam, and its publication marked the start of what ultimately became an Islamist slippery slope. The resolution asserts that "sovereignty belongs to Allah" (not the people), and tasks the state with the role of enabling Muslims "to order their lives in both the individual and collective spheres in accordance with the teachings of Islam."[5] These core resolution principles had virtually nothing in common with the secular views of

Pakistan's founding fathers. Instead, they were more aligned with the views of Islamist ideologues like Maulana Abul Ala Maududi, the founder of the Jamaat-e-Islami.

Maulana Maududi had not been an early supporter of the foundation of Pakistan mainly because of his aversion toward the largely secular leadership of the Muslim League. Yet Maududi changed his views soon after Pakistan's creation, and came to see the new majority Muslim state as a *tabula rasa* on which his ideal of an Islamic "theo-democracy" might be implemented.[6] Historically, the Jamaat-e-Islami has been unable to win enough electoral support to fully implement Maududi's ideas. But the Islamist organization has over the decades sought to penetrate into and align itself with the country's military and civilian bureaucratic establishment. For their part, secular leaders in the military as well as civil bureaucracies have generally believed that they could accommodate the ideas of Islamists like Maududi without having to cede formal political space to them.

Over the years, civilian and military leaders have thus defended the idea that Pakistan was established on the basis of Islamic ideology and that the purpose of the state was to implement and safeguard this ideology. Pakistan's first Prime Minister Liaquat Ali Khan, for example, spoke frequently about a special "Pakistani ideology" and about the primary importance of Islam within this national ideology. General Ayub Khan—who, as army commander in chief, played an influential role in Pakistan's early politics and ultimately became the country's first military ruler from 1958-1969—reaffirmed this view that Pakistan was created on the foundation of Islamic ideology. He also believed that the state's primary duty was to fully implement these Islamic ideals but that the Pakistani state had not lived up to its responsibilities and the nation suffered as a consequence. As General Ayub put it, man's "greatest yearning is for an ideology for which he should be able to lay down his life," and for Pakistanis, that ideology was "obviously Islam." He stated further that it "was on that basis [of Islam] that we fought for and got Pakistan, but having got it, we failed to order our lives in accordance with it."[7]

General Ayub's views would be reinforced by another military ruler, General Zia ul Haq, who launched a sweeping state-led Islamization agenda in the late 1970s that fundamentally reshaped the country's major institutions, politics, and culture. In General Zia's view, "the ideology of Pakistan is Islam and only Islam. There should be no misunderstanding on this score. We should in all sincerity accept Islam as Pakistan's basic ideology ... otherwise ... this country (will) be exposed to secular ideologies."[8]

IN 1956, PAKISTAN WAS OFFICIALLY RENAMED THE "ISLAMIC REPUBLIC OF PAKISTAN," and since then the evolution of Islamic politics and an Islamic national identity within the country has been consistently encouraged and enforced by state policy. This is especially apparent in how modern Pakistani leaders have sought to use religion to unify the nation. A key challenge facing the country's founders was that each one of Pakistan's principal ethnic groups overlapped national borders and extended into neighboring countries. Without a common national identity, there was little reason why the country's inhabitants should prefer to be Pakistanis and why the country as a whole should cohere.

The solution offered in subsequent years has been to emphasize the shared Islamic religion of all of Pakistan's peoples over other attributes of national distinctiveness. This desire to create "one nation, one language, one religion" (a common slogan in Pakistani political life) has manifested itself in an effort to suppress local, ethno-linguistic identities by the state and a related effort to replace these identities with a national identity rooted in Islam.

In practice, unifying Pakistan on the basis of religious nationalism has proven to be an unattainable goal. It has, however, been the justification of immense political violence. While many factors led to the break-up of West and East Pakistan and the creation of Bangladesh in 1971, Bengali resentment over the suppression of their ethno-linguistic identity played a vital role. This is because Pakistan's army was and remains mainly Punjabi-Pashtun at the soldier level and Punjabi-Muhajir-Pashtun in the officer corps.[9] Similarly, Punjabis and Muhajirs occupy a disproportionate number of posts in Pakistan's civil services in terms of their percentage of the population in Pakistan. Before 1971, one of the key grievances of the Bengali majority was that Bengalis constituted only seven percent of the army and four percent of the civil service. After 1971, for many Baluchis, Sindhis, and to some extent even Pashtuns, the Pakistani identity represented Punjabi-Muhajir chauvinism.

The Indian Muslim elite who founded Pakistan came to view their new country as the rightful homeland of all of the Muslims of the subcontinent, and they urged India's Muslims to immigrate to the new country. However, they faced many challenges on this front, not least because Pakistan shared common history and deep cultural linkages with India. The new country thus had little history of its own to appeal to that could serve as the basis for a new national identity.

Furthermore, the 1947 partition of the British Raj into India and Pakistan separated the new Pakistani state from the heart of the historical Muslim empire in South Asia, which later became part of predominantly Hindu India. Pakistan had little within its new territory to connect its people to the rich cultural heritage of South Asian Islamic traditions. Moreover, the fact that over one-third of South Asia's Muslims remained in India after partition meant that Pakistan from the beginning was hard put to justify itself as the homeland for South Asia's Muslims. Pakistani efforts to construct an Islamic nationalist identity were complicated further in 1971, when an additional one-third of South Asia's Muslims sought autonomy from Pakistan and created the separate country of Bangladesh.

The architects of Pakistani nationalist identity might have addressed these dilemmas in one of two ways. On the one hand, they might have acknowledged Pakistan's essentially

Indian history, but this would have exposed the new state to a critique of its *raison d'etre* and motivations for breaking politically with India. Alternatively, they could have crafted a new historical narrative that supported Pakistan's modern ambitions and identity. Pakistani nationalist leaders opted for the latter course, and in doing so began a still ongoing search for episodic evidence in the history of Indian Islam that could be used to justify Pakistan's creation and its continued existence as a separate Islamic state. Constructing a new national ideology thus involved fabricating an entirely new historical narrative. Needless to say, this new historical narrative has not always conformed to historical facts.

The official history of Pakistan reinforces the popular belief that the country wasn't created in 1947, but rather twelve centuries earlier when Islam was first introduced to India as a result of the annexation of Sindh in 712 CE by the Arab-Muslim Umayyad Empire. The shared history of the peoples of South Asia has been rewritten in Pakistan's school curricula to stress the fundamental difference and divergence between Hindus and Muslims. The thirteen centuries since the conquest of Sindh are described in Pakistani school textbooks as the struggle of Muslims to maintain their distinctiveness, and the creation of an independent Pakistan is seen as the culmination of that struggle. This ideology-based narrative has been championed both by secular as well as religious elements in Pakistan, and the "Pakistan Studies" curriculum that is based on this narrative is taught in secular schools as well as religious establishments.[10]

Despite the tumultuous political history of Pakistan, each one of the country's constitutions—including those of 1956, 1962, 1973, and even the legal framework orders adopted under military rule—has consistently reaffirmed the Islamic identity of the state and asserted that no law in the country should contravene any of the tenets of Islam. By far the most extreme and harsh policies of Islamization took place under General Zia ul Haq, who ruled from 1977-89 and oversaw a broad-based effort to reorder Pakistani society according to a new Islamic vision that transformed the legal system, the education system, and the military.

During General Zia's rule, it became the norm to treat a religious degree from a madrasa as an equivalent of the professional and academic degrees awarded by modern universities and colleges. This shift contributed to the gradual Islamization of the lower ranks of the civil service and bureaucracy. Moreover, the professionals who entered the higher ranks of government, media, and academia were also subjected to years of government-sponsored "Pakistan Studies" and religious studies (*Islamiyat*). Over time, these educational initiatives produced a bureaucratic class whose worldview was deeply influenced by a politicized understanding of Islam, and there were few in the position to challenge or disagree with their ideas. Ultimately, this indoctrination led this traditionally secular and liberal group of professionals to become ever more supportive of Islamist principles shaping government policy.

The Pakistani military and its culture were also fundamentally transformed by

General Zia's Islamization policies. In General Zia's view, Pakistani military was to serve as the "guardian" of both the "ideological as well as geographical frontiers" of the country.[11] The military adopted recruitment and advancement practices that favored those who showed themselves to be religiously and ideologically committed to Pakistan's Islamic identity. Additionally, compulsory prayers and Islamic classes, many of them taught by Deobandi and Jamaat-e-Islami religious leaders who preached a radical version of Islam, became routine within the military.

The military thus became an increasingly religious and ideologically-driven organization, and this remains very much the case today. For example, in August 2009, on the eve of Pakistan's 62nd Independence Anniversary, Chief of Army Staff General Ashfaq Pervez Kayani stated that "Islam is the soul and spirit of Pakistan. It is our strength and we will always be an Islamic republic." Further, General Kayani emphasized that the Pakistani army would continue to defend the country "against all internal and external threats."[12] This has been apparent in the country's foreign-policy agendas, which, from the anti-Soviet jihad in Afghanistan to the ongoing strategic competition with "Hindu India," have all become invested in profound ideological and theological significance. In February 2010, General Kayani stated that his views are "India-centric," reflecting the common view within the Pakistan army that India is the primary national security threat.[13] This perception has clearly been reinforced by Pakistan's Islam-based ideology, and it has become more prevalent in recent years as the military itself has become a more ideological institution.

On the other hand, it must also be acknowledged that India is not perceived as the primary threat by everyone within the Pakistan military or, for that matter, the public at large. In May 2011, Husain Haqqani, Pakistan's Ambassador to the United States, observed in a talk at the Islamabad–based National Defense University that only a small minority within the military sees India as the primary threat. For other officers, the greatest threat to national security is posed either by domestic jihadist movements or by the United States. Moreover, the army's leadership has repeatedly expressed deep concern over the recent ethno-linguistic clashes in Karachi, and some political parties have called for military intervention to restore order in the city.[14]

GOVERNMENT POLICIES AND EDUCATIONAL CURRICULA, WHICH HAVE BEEN designed to create a unified nation by championing Islam at home and pan-Islamism abroad, have made it increasingly difficult for the government to control or subdue groups that justify violence against the perceived enemies of Islam. In fact, because it derives so much of its identity and legitimacy from Islam, the Pakistani state has frequently succumbed to Islamist demands on a range of social and other questions.

This clearly has been the case in the plight of the Ahmadis, a minority Muslim sect considered to be non-Muslim by most orthodox and conservative Muslims.[15] In the early 1950s, a political rivalry between two factions of the Muslim League led the Punjab Chief Minister, Mian Mumtaz Daulatana, to instigate street riots, with help from Islamist groups like the Jamaat-e-Islami, demanding an official declaration of Ahmadis as non-Muslims.[16] The goal was to force the resignation of the foreign minister, Mr. Zafrulla Khan, an Ahmadi, and henceforth overthrow the federal government. (This process has become a recurring phenomenon in Pakistan: certain vested interests—political parties or individuals—try to use street power, especially that of the Islamist groups, to apply pressure on the elected government. Situations often escalate uncontrollably and the military must consequently be called in to restore order.)

Soon after the anti-Ahmadi riots erupted, a court of inquiry presided over by Justice Muhammad Munir (later Chief Justice of Pakistan) was set up, and the court submitted its final report in 1954. The following comments by Justice Munir reflect the fundamental problem of "Whose Islam?" the modern Islamic state of Pakistan has struggled to answer through its politics:

> Keeping in view the several definitions given by the ulama, need we make any comment except that no two learned divines are agreed on this fundamental. If we attempt our own definition as each learned divine has done and that definition differs from that given by all others, we unanimously go out of the fold of Islam. And if we adopt the definition given by any one of the ulama, we remain Muslims according to the view of that alim but kafirs according to the definition of everyone else.[17]

The Ahmadi issue flared up again in the 1970s under the government of Pakistan's first democratically elected civilian Prime Minister, Zulfikar Ali Bhutto. A clash between Ahmadi and Islamist students in Punjab resulted in massive, street-wide riots that threatened Mr. Bhutto's government. Despite being a secular, western-oriented politician, Mr. Bhutto ultimately acquiesced to the Islamist Pakistani identity and narrative. Facing constant challenges from both Islamists and other elements, Bhutto began efforts to Islamize his domestic policies in an effort to save his government.

In 1974, Pakistan's national constitution was amended to declare Ahmadis officially non-Muslims. The government at the time thought it had resolved the Ahmadi issue, but in reality this was only the beginning of a long struggle. Both Muslim sects and non-Muslim minorities continue to be targeted by Islamist groups.

Bhutto had already been a champion of pan-Islamism in Pakistan's external relations. In January 1972, Bhutto embarked on what was called the "Journey of Resistance": a 10,000-mile goodwill trip to Iran, Turkey, Morocco, Tunisia, Libya, Algeria, Egypt, and Syria. In May and June of 1972, Bhutto also went to Saudi Arabia, Kuwait, United Arab

Emirates, Iraq, Lebanon, Jordan, Ethiopia, Mauritania, Guinea, Nigeria, Sudan and So-malia. Though these trips had political and economic aims, the key objective was sym-bolic and meant to bolster the Islamic self-image and confidence of the Pakistani people following the trauma of losing control over Bangladesh in 1971.

Moreover, by orienting Pakistan toward the Muslim Middle East, the Bhutto govern-ment sought to provide Pakistan with a new Islamic Middle Eastern identity that would allow it to escape its Indian history and identity. Bhutto's trips to the Middle East were also helpful in obtaining economic aid for Pakistan's nuclear weapons program. Libya and the Gulf Sates provided Pakistan with the much-needed monetary support for this ambitious program. In return Bhutto often referred to Pakistan's bomb as the "Islamic bomb."[18]

While the Pakistani state has struggled to rein in Islamism, it has also often condoned and encouraged Islamist groups by providing them with covert support. The state, and especially the Pakistani military-intelligence establishment, has sought to establish ties with these Islamist groups and enlist them in pursuit of its domestic and foreign policy agendas.

In the domestic arena, Islamist groups helped curtail the influence of secular and liberal forces, political parties and others who backed ethno-linguistic identities (e.g., Bengalis, Sindhis, Baluchis, Pashtuns). During the 1971 conflict in East Pakistan, Jamaat-e-Islami militias fought alongside the Pakistani regular army to help suppress Muslims. They subsequently renounced the new state of Bangladesh as a form of national apostasy.

Sectarianism and violent sectarian conflict in Pakistan can also be tied to specific poli-cies implemented by the government. As part of his policy of Islamization in 1979, Gen-eral Zia imposed a system by which the state would automatically deduct *zakat* from the bank accounts and salaries of all Muslims.[19] This outraged many in Pakistan's minor-ity Shia population, since they customarily offer their charity money to their individ-ual clerics. Newly formed Shia organizations such as the Tehrik-e-Nifaz-Fiqh-e-Jaafariya (TNFJ) subsequently laid siege to the capital city of Islamabad.

In response to this Shiite activism, elements in the Pakistani state began to provide support to Sunni radical and militant organizations to confront the Shia. Driven by a mix of political, economic, and religious factors, sectarian conflict has continued to plague Pakistan, and the Saudi Arabian and Iranian establishments have also used the conflict to enact a proxy war. (Nowadays, Pakistan's leading anti-Shiite organizations are the Sipaha-e-Sahaba Pakistan and its breakaway militant group, Lashkar-e-Jhangvi. Sipaha-e-Sahaba subscribes to Deobandi views and has close ties to the Jamiat-e-Ulema Islam, a Deobandi religious organization. The leading Shiite radical group is the TNFJ and its militant off-shoot is the Sipaha-e-Muhammad Pakistan.)

The impact of the government's use of Islamist groups to suppress non-Islamic identities is clearly visible in Pakistan today. In 1947, non-Muslim minorities including

Ahmadis, Hindus, Christians, Sikhs, and Parsees accounted for twenty-five percent of Pakistan's total population; by 2010, this number had shrunk to five percent of the country's population. Hindus and Christians together comprise around four percent of the Pakistani population. While Hindus face discrimination on religious grounds, the conflict-ridden relationship between India and Pakistan has also caused them to be treated as 'fifth columnists' and potential enemies of the state. As 'People of the Book,' the Christian minority was traditionally tolerated in Pakistan. Over the last few decades, however, attacks on Christians have escalated. Moreover, the harsh blasphemy law enacted during General Zia's regime has often been used to target the Christian minority.

Meanwhile, in the foreign policy arena, Islamist groups and their militant off-shoots have helped the Pakistani state fight asymmetrical covert wars with both of Pakistan's immediate neighbors, India and Afghanistan. A majority of the Islamist militant groups operating in Indian-administered Kashmir have ties with Pakistani Islamist groups, and Pakistan's military-intelligence establishment views these groups as proxies to help suppress a larger adversarial neighbor. Similarly, state support for Islamist groups and militias operating in Afghanistan serves both domestic and foreign policy goals, which include subduing Pashtun irredentism and setting up a pro-Pakistan, Pashtun-led Afghan government. As a leading Pakistani scholar, Khaled Ahmed, states, "Intolerance is embedded in the evolution of the Islamic state," and that is the foundation of Pakistani intolerance.[20]

Despite the deaths of over 10,000 civilians and almost 4,000 security personnel in the fight against terrorism since 2003, a Pew poll conducted in June 2011 discovered that the majority of Pakistanis still see India as a greater threat to Pakistan than jihadist organizations.[21] Even after thousands of Pakistanis have been killed by jihadist groups, conspiracy theories abound, with some claiming that the terrorists are in fact foreign mercenaries because Muslims would never kill fellow Muslims. The national press, too, has often contributed to the growing delusion and zealotry in the country's political discourse. For example, Majid Nizami, who runs *The Nation-Nawa-i-Waqt* media group, has stated publicly that the only way for Pakistan to obtain Kashmir from India is to start a nuclear war, and he has offered to be "tied to a nuclear bomb" and get "dropped on India."[22] Meanwhile, Hafiz Saeed, the former head of the jihadist group Lashkar-e-Taiba (which is responsible for a number of terror attacks including the 2008 attacks on Mumbai, India), is presently under house arrest and yet still able to speak openly about jihad against India while receiving little censure from the public and government.[23]

Opposing "Hindu India" has become a defining feature of the Pakistani Islamic nationalist narrative. Without an identity that is firmly anti-Indian, Pakistan's leaders fear their country will be reabsorbed within a greater Indian identity—with potentially irreversible political and strategic consequences. As Khaled Ahmed observed in 2008, "It appears natural to people that to be 'Pakistani' you have to be anti-Hindu: it is part of the definition, like the core of the being. You have to define yourself in opposition to the other. India has become the definite other for the Pakistanis."

WHEN PAKISTAN WAS CREATED, THE COUNTRY'S DIVERSE INHABITANTS had little in the way of a common identity that might bind them together. Indeed, even the very idea of Pakistan—which emerged in the 1930s, as some Indian Muslims began their quest for a separate homeland—had a relatively short history. Pakistan's politicians have struggled with this lack of a common identity and principles ever since. As early as 1956 Hans Morgenthau presciently noted, "Pakistan is not a nation and hardly a state. It has no justification in history, ethnic origin, language, civilization, or the consciousness of those who make up its population ... Thus it is hard to see how anything but a miracle, or else a revival of religious fanaticism, will assure Pakistan's future."[24]

Pakistan's early generation undertook to establish their new state and nation on the basis of Islamic ideology. This ideology-based national identity soon became the defining force of Pakistani politics, and it was accepted by both secular and Islamist parts of Pakistani society. As a Pakistani scholar, Waheed-uz-Zaman, noted in 1973:

> the wish to see the kingdom of God established in a Muslim territory
> ...was the moving idea behind the demand for Pakistan, the corner-stone
> of the movement, the ideology of the people, and the *raison d'etre* of
> the new nation-state.... If we let go the ideology of Islam, we cannot hold
> together as a nation by any other means.... If the Arabs, the Turks, the
> Iranians, God forbid, give up Islam, the Arabs yet remain Arabs, the Turks
> remain Turks, the Iranians remain Iranians, but what do we remain if
> we give up Islam?[25]

To be religious is one thing, and to use it to run a state is quite another. Instead of binding the nation together, Pakistan's grounding in Islamic ideology has actually operated to divide the Pakistani nation, pitting Muslim against non-Muslim, and Muslim against Muslim. If Pakistan is to survive, it will have to do away with its reliance on Islamic ideology and find a new basis for the state and nation.

When Pakistan was created not all of the new country's leaders were in favor of constructing a national identity on the basis of Islamic ideology. Huseyn Shaheed Suhrawardy, a leading Indian Muslim who would later serve as Pakistan's Prime Minister, advocated a territorial-based national identity; unfortunately, his views never gained sufficient favor or support. A Pakistani nationalism and identity along the lines proposed by Suhrawardy—which is defined territorially and is accepting of ethno-linguistic differences domestically as well as the common history and enduring affinities that Pakistan shares with its South Asian neighbors—would help Pakistan move forward. This would, however, require the national narrative, including school curricula, to be dramatically rewritten so that it has more in common with facts and reality. This outcome will inevitably prove difficult to achieve, especially since so many of the country's civilian and military leaders have over the years embraced the Islamist narrative of Pakistan's origins and purpose.

NOTES

1. British Council Pakistan. *The Next Generation*. Full report available at http://www.britishcouncil.pk/pakistan-Next-Generation-Report.pdf.
2. Gilani Research Foundation. *Religion and Governance: Islamization of Society*. Full report available at http://www.gallup.com.pk/Polls/31-05-11.pdf.
3. Ayesha Jalal. *The Sole Spokesman: Jinnah, the Muslim League and the Demand for Pakistan* (Cambridge: Cambridge University Press. 1994).
4. Jamil u-Din Ahmad (ed), *Speeches and Writings of Mr Jinnah*, Vol I, Lahore: Ashraf, 1960, p 241-243. Cited in K.B. Sayeed, *op cit,* p 199.
5. *The Objectives Resolution of Pakistan, 1949.*
6. The Jamaat e Islami was founded in 1941 by Maulana Abul Ala Maududi. Maududi believed that Islam was not just a religion and faith but a way of life. Maududi's ideal political system was a "theo-democracy" which meant "limited people's sovereignty under the suzerainty of God."
7. Muhammad Ayub Khan, *Friends Not Masters: A political autobiography*, Karachi, Oxford University Press, 1967, pp.196-197.
8. "The President on Pakistan's Ideological Basis," Address by President General Zia-ul-Haq at the inauguration of Shariat Faculty at the Quaid-i-Azam University, Islamabad, 8 October 1979 Islamabad: Ministry of Information and Broadcasting, n.d., p. 2. Cited in C.G.P. Rakisits, "Center Province Relations in Pakistan under President Zia: The Government's and Opposition's Approaches," *Pacific Affairs*, Vol 61(1), 1988, p 79.
9. Muhajir is a term which in the Indian subcontinent refers to those Urdu-speaking Indian Muslims—from Muslim minority provinces—who migrated from India to Pakistan at the time of Partition. Though many Bengali and Punjabi Muslims also migrated across the border but most of them settled down in Pakistani Punjab and Bengal and are not normally referred to as Muhajirs.
10. See Mubashir Hasan. :The Mirage of Power": An Inquiry Into the Bhutto Years, 1971-1977 (Karachi. Oxford University Press. 2000) p 202-208.
11. For detailed analysis of textbooks in various subjects please look at the following report titled 'Subtle Subversion' http://www.uvm.edu/~envprog/madrassah/TextbooksinPakistan.pdf.
12. Speech given to the graduates at the Officers Training Academy at Kakul, *Pakistan Times*, April 14, 1978.
13. "We are against terrorism, not religion, says Kayani." *Dawn*, August 14, 2009.
14. "Pakistan will remain India-centric: Kayani." *Hindustan Times*, February 5, 2010.

15. "Army concerned about Karachi situation: ISPR." *Daily Times Pakistan,* September 4, 2011.

16. Ahmadis or Ahmadiyyas follow the teachings of a 19th century messiah Mirza Ghulam Ahmad—whom they consider a prophet—and their two main points of disagreement are that they do not acknowledge the finality of the Prophet Muhammad and do not accept the obligation of jihad.

17. Full details of the 1953 riots are taken from the following report. *Report on the Court of Inquiry constituted under Punjab Act II of 1954 to enquire into the Punjab disturbances of 1953* (Lahore, Government Printing Press, 1954).

18. "We know that Israel and South Africa have full nuclear capability. The Christian, Jewish and Hindu civilizations have this capability. The communist powers also possess it. Only the Islamic civilization was without it, but that position was about to change." Taken from Zulfikar Ali Bhutto, *If I am Assassinated*, New Delhi: Vikas Publishing House, 1979, p 138.

19. *Zakat*—One of the Five Pillars of Islam dealing with the giving of a fixed portion of one's wealth to charity, generally to the poor and needy.

20. Khaled Ahmed, "Roots of our Intolerance," http://tribune.com.pk/story/173247/roots-of-our-intolerance/ May 22, 2011, *Express Tribune.*

21. Pew Global Attitudes Project Poll, June 21, 2011.
http://pewglobal.org/2011/06/21/u-s-image-in-pakistan-falls-no-further-following-bin-laden-killing/.

22. Shakil Chaudhary. "*Media Baron wants India to be defeated in a nuclear war,*" June 25, 2010.
http://www.viewpointonline.net/Old/fullstory.php?t=Media%20baron%20wants%20India%20to%20be%20defeated%20in%20a%20nuclear%20war&f=full-8-june-25.php&y=2010&m=june.

23. "JuD chief back to criticizing India," *The Economic Times.* July 26, 2009; Nirupama Subramanian. 'FIR on what Hafiz Saeed said' *The Hindu* September 19, 2009.

24. Hans J. Morgenthau, "Military illusions," *The New Republic*, March 19, 1956, p. 15-16.

25. Waheed-uz-Zarnan, "Editor's Note," in "The Quest for Identity," Proceedings of The First Congress on the History and Culture of Pakistan, University of Islamabad, April 1973. Islamabad: University of Islamabad Press, 1974, p. i. Cited in William Richter, "The Political Dynamics of Islamic Resurgence in Pakistan," *Asian Survey*, Vol 19(6), 1979, p. 549.

The Assertion of Barelvi Extremism

By Ismail Khan

O N JANUARY 4, 2011, SALMAN TASEER, THE GOVERNOR OF THE PAKISTANI province of Punjab, was shot to death in the capital city of Islamabad by one of his bodyguards, Malik Mumtaz Qadri. In his confession statement, Qadri said that he committed the cold-blooded murder to avenge the governor's public criticism of Pakistan's blasphemy law.[1] The controversial law provides for punishments, ranging from fines to death sentences, for those found guilty of desecrating religion.[2] Governor Taseer emerged as an outspoken critic of the law through his advocacy of leniency in the case of Aasia Bibi, a poor Christian woman convicted to death on November 11, 2010 for allegedly speaking "ill" against the Prophet Muhammad (a charge that Aasia flatly rejected.)[3] As she waited in prison to be hanged for her offense, Taseer personally visited her and forwarded her clemency appeal to the President of Pakistan.[4] The governor's efforts on Aasia's behalf—and his labeling of the blasphemy law as a "black law"—outraged many in Pakistan. By late November 2010, religious groups around the country were staging mass demonstrations against the government to show support for the law and to condemn Taseer, with some claiming that the governor himself was guilty of apostasy—a crime punishable by death in Islamic law.[5]

While the high-profile assassination shocked many in Pakistan, not all condemned the murder. Indeed, thousands rallied to Qadri's defense, praising him as a hero for his "religious honor and integrity."[6] A Facebook page honoring Qadri was created only hours after the murder and soon attracted over a thousand followers; similar websites praising the assassin remain active to this day.[7] A few days after the assassination, leading religious groups led a demonstration of over fifty thousand people in Karachi in support of the blasphemy law. During the rally, Qadri was lionized as a Muslim hero, while rally leaders sternly warned the crowds against mourning Taseer, whom they claimed had deviated from Islam. When Qadri was later led to trial in Islamabad, a group of lawyers chanted slogans in support of him; a month after that, students sent flowers and cards to Qadri on Valentine's Day to show their affection.[8]

Scholars from virtually all of the country's Islamic sects, despite the festering theological and sectarian disputes between them, were unanimous in their backing of the blasphemy law. But the response of scholars from the mainstream Barelvi school of thought to the Taseer assassination was especially hardline—with some Barelvi leaders expressly condoning the slaying. This stance came as a surprise to many, since the Barelvi school to which the majority of Pakistan's Sunni Muslims adheres enjoys a reputation for moderation, not least because Barelvi scholars have been at the forefront in refuting the puritanical ideologies that have been linked in recent years to rising sectarianism and terrorism.

Yet, two days after Taseer's murder, over five hundred Barelvi scholars from an organization called the Jamaat Ahl-e-Sunnat Pakistan (JASP) issued a statement that explicitly warned mosque leaders not to offer Islamic funeral prayers to Salman Taseer.[9] "No Muslim," declared the JASP in its statement, "should attend the funeral or even try to pray for Salman Taseer or even express any kind of regret or sympathy over the incident." As an umbrella group that forms the largest body of Barelvi scholars, the JASP's decisions are widely respected and accepted by other Barelvis—and most, indeed, appeared to pay heed.[10] In Lahore, the Punjab capital where Taseer was to be buried, the Imam of Badshahi Mosque refused to lead ritual services for the dead governor.[11] Subsequently, "cleric after cleric" refused to lead the funeral prayer for the murdered governor, according to Taseer's daughter,[12] and other Barelvi organizations reportedly annulled Taseer's marriage to show they no longer considered him a Muslim.

Still other Barelvi scholars rushed to Qadri's defense. Instead of condemning the murderer, one scholar suggested it was the understandable reaction of a pious man against Taseer's contemptible actions to undermine a law to protect the sanctity of the Prophet Muhammad.[13] Moreover, since the Pakistan constitution provides high ranking officials immunity from criminal prosecution,[14] others argued the vigilante slaying was the only way to punish the governor for his crimes against Islam; Qadri really had no choice in the matter.[15]

As Qadri's trial began, a leading Barelvi organization called the Sunni Tehreek threatened to blockade the national parliament should Qadri be sentenced to death.[16] On October 1, 2011, when a Pakistani court sentenced Qadri to death for his crime, Sunni Tehreek announced it would organize a round of protests against the verdict of the court. Unlike JASP, which serves as a platform for esteemed religious scholars, Sunni Tehreek has been characterized as a grassroots "religious force" that has been organized to actively "defend the interests of the Barelvi school of thought." In recent times, the organization has emerged as a key player in Pakistan's sectarian feuds, and it is widely expected that the movement will compete in future political elections as well.

The assassin himself never had a personal history with Islamist extremism. In fact, Qadri claimed to have acted entirely alone, and he strongly denied being influenced by any of the radical political or religious movements known for fomenting jihad within Pakistan. He confessed that he made up his mind to kill the governor only three days before, on December 31, 2010. That day had been a Friday, the Muslim holy day, and across the country local mosque leaders had reignited large demonstrations against the repeal of the blasphemy law. A devout Muslim, and a member of the Barelvi proselytizing organization known as the Dawat-e-Islami, Qadri himself attended a rally that took place in Rawalpindi to show his support for the blasphemy law. He later confessed that he had been inspired to murder the governor by the "rousing speeches" and prayers delivered by the rally's clerical leaders.[17] One of those clerics was Hanif Qureshi, a notoriously fiery and charismatic Barelvi scholar-activist and founder of an organization called Shahab-e-Islam. After Taseer's murder, Qureshi dedicated a sermon to honor Qadri, and also led a procession to the assassin's house.[18]

As the myriad connections between Qadri and the mainstream Barelvi school of thought came to light, it soon gave way to new worries about the further ingress of radical ideas into society. The outpouring of Barelvi support for Qadri, after all, showed that this could not simply be treated as an isolated act by a deranged individual. Concerns for what this meant for Pakistan's struggle with terrorism were especially acute because the Barelvis are seen by many as the moderate Islamic antidote to Islamist militancy. In fact, the current government led by the Pakistan People's Party (Taseer himself was a PPP politician) has actively courted Barelvis as part of their counter-radicalization efforts. Known for their orthodox piety and folksy, Sufi-leaning religious practices, Barelvis have generally eschewed violence and vigilantism. In recent times, Barelvi scholars have led the way among religious groups in tackling what they have decried as the "Talibanization" of Pakistani society. They have issued fatwas against suicide bombing as well as learned refutations of the puritanical Islamic ideologies such as Deobandism that have been linked in recent years to rising sectarianism and terrorism.

Yet the case of Mumtaz Qadri and the scale of the Barelvi support for him has rattled many of these popular conceptions about Barelvi moderation—just as it has raised new worries over Pakistan's struggle with Islamist militancy. As *The Washington Post* reported,

> While many factions have lauded the slaying [of Governor Taseer], the peace-promoting Barelvi sect has spearheaded mass rallies to demand the release of the assassin, a policeman. Because most Pakistanis are Barelvis, their stance is challenging the belief long held among liberals here—and hoped for by nervous U.S. officials—that the Muslim majority in this nuclear-armed nation is more moderate than militant.[19]

What accounts for the Barelvi school of thought's seemingly incoherent, even paradoxical stance against the militancy of the Taliban on the one hand, and its broad endorsement of the killing of Governor Taseer on the other? To understand the Barelvi response to Taseer's assassination, it must be situated within the broader context of Pakistan's religious politics and the sectarian struggle among competing Islamic movements. This dynamic has contributed to the rise in recent years of new forms of Barelvi activism and communalist assertion, some of which have expressed themselves in militancy, and which will be crucial to understanding the future of Pakistan's fight with Islamist ideology and militancy as a whole.

The Formation of Barelvi Thought

"BARELVI ISLAM" OR "BARELVISM" IS A SUNNI ISLAMIC MOVEMENT AND SCHOOL OF thought that is widespread among the Muslim populations of South Asia, as well as within the South Asian Diaspora. The name "Barelvi" itself traces its root to the Indian town of Bareilly, which was the birthplace (and thereby the last name) of Ahmed Raza Khan Bareilly, a pioneering scholar and revivalist of the latter half of the nineteenth century whose teachings greatly influenced modern religious thought across the subcontinent. Because of Ahmed Raza's prestige as a scholar, Barelvis do not necessarily object to being popularly identified with his teachings. As a formal matter, however, Barelvis are quick to point out that they are not disciples of a nineteenth-century teaching, but rather they are orthodox Sunnis, or "Ahl-e-Sunnat wal Jamaat" (Followers of the Traditions of the Prophet and Congregation) who adhere to true Islam as it was originally practiced by the Prophet and his companions as well as by various saints (wali) throughout history.[20] Ahmed Raza is seen as a great reviver and defender of Islam as it was originally revealed, and for this reason Barelvis commonly describe him as the "Imam of the Ahl-e-Sunnat."[21]

Barelvis also describe themselves as "Ahl-e-Sunnat" (a shortened version of the formal term) so as to distinguish themselves from their ideological rivals, which include most prominently the Deobandis. Deobandi Islam, like Barelvism, also emerged during the latter half of the nineteenth century in British-occupied India as a movement of revival and reform. While both of these Islamic movements adhere to the Hanafi school of jurisprudence, Barelvis and Deobandis follow sharply divergent doctrines and practices. Although the two movements have from time to time found common cause, their historical relationship has mostly been bitter and frequently violent.

Barelvism originally emerged as a reaction against the propagation of several new streams of Islamic thought—including, though not limited to, the Deobandis. Ahmed Raza himself painstakingly developed refutations of Deobandism, the Ahl-e-Hadith (whom the Barelvis have decried as the "Wahhabis" of South Asia), as well as the minority Ahmadi sect.[22] What has conventionally distinguished the Barelvis from the Deobandis and Ahl-e-Hadith is the latter two's notoriously puritan understanding and austere practice of Islam, which the Barelvis reject as unorthodox.

While performing the Hajj in 1906, Ahmed Raza asked the *ulemas* of Mecca and Medina to endorse his fatwas and refutations of the teachings of Deobandis and other new schools of thought in South Asia. (Mecca and Medina were then under Ottoman rule, and the authority of the religious scholars in these two holy cities was at the time recognized across the Islamic world.) The Arab scholars, according to the Barelvis, agreed fully with Ahmed Raza's propositions, and a total of twenty clerics from Mecca and thirteen from Medina endorsed *Hussam al-Harmain*, a book of fatwas compiled by Ahmed Raza.[23] Most of these fatwas concern what constitutes the proper veneration of the Prophet Muhammad, and by these standards, Ahmed Raza accused the Deobandis of not bestowing sufficient respect upon the Prophet—and thus, found them guilty of heresy.

After Ahmed Raza returned from Arabia to India, his anti-Deobandi fatwas began to circulate, and this put the puritan Deobandis on edge. The Deobandi scholars reacted by developing their own refutations of Ahmed Raza's teachings, accusing the Barelvi movement as well of heresy. This launched what came to be known as the "Fatwa War" between the Barelvis and Deobandis. From 1925 until now it has been claimed a virtually "uncountable" number of fatwas were issued by Barelvi and Deobandi scholars renouncing the other school of thought for their deviant, "un-Islamic" beliefs and practices. These fatwas have addressed a range of matters—from religion to politics, both great and small—and they have only further divided the two schools of thoughts on nearly every issue.

One of the effects of this now century-old feud has been the institutionalization of the rivalry between the two Sunni schools. This rivalry has been as much political as it has been theological, and, since the two groups accuse each other of heresy, it has frequently led to violence. The more inclusive Barelvis have borne the brunt of this. In 1979, for instance, an intense *manazira*, or one-on-one theological debate, between a Barelvi and a Deobandi scholar was held in the Punjabi town of Jhang. Known as the "Manazira-e-Jhang," the debate lasted for seven to eight hours.[24] The Deobandi participant in the debate, Haq Nawaz Jhangvi, would later form an infamous militant organization called Sipah-e-Sahaba, which has since earned notoriety for killing Shiites, Barelvis and minorities throughout Pakistan.

Today, Barelvis commonly believe that the original manifestos of the founders of Sipah-e-Sahaba as well as Lashkar-e-Taiba (whose Ahl-e-Hadith ideology resembles al-Qaeda's ideology, and which is responsible for the 2008 Mumbai attacks among other attacks), reveal that both organizations were set up principally to wage war on the Barelvis and their shrines.[25] While evidence suggests this is a revisionist belief (both militant groups had other declared foes, not only Barelvis), the fact that this belief is so widespread among Barelvis reveals the degree to which they feel they are targeted and besieged by these Deobandi organizations.

It is understandable that Barelvis should feel this way. In recent years, Deobandi militant organizations like Sipah-e-Sahaba-Pakistan and its splinter militia, Lashkar-e-Jhangvi, have serially attacked not only Shiites, but also Barelvis. These Islamists have seized Barelvi mosques, attacked their shrines and targeted their scholars. There have been numerous attacks on Barelvi and Shiite processions honoring the birth of Ali (son-in-law of Muhammad), Hussain (grandson of Muhammad), and even the Prophet in different parts of Pakistan. In 2010, there were additional attacks on prominent Barelvi shrines such as the Data Ganj Bakhsh in Lahore and Abdullah Shah Ghazi in Karachi. Indeed, what is commonly perceived as a sectarian conflict between Sunni and Shia Muslims in Pakistan is more accurately understood as a conflict between Deobandis and puritanical Islamic schools on the one hand, and the Shia and Barelvi communities on the other.

Between March 2005 and April 2011 alone, one independent study has counted as many as twenty-nine attacks on Barelvi shrines.[26] Moreover, in 2009, a suicide bomber from the Tehreek-e-Taliban, a Deobandi movement, was responsible for the assassination of the leading Barelvi scholar Mufti Sarfraz Naeemi, who became well-known for his anti-Taliban teachings.[27] Barelvis commonly point to the "Nishtar Park Tragedy" of 2006 as a prime example of the Deobandi effort to eliminate Barelvism entirely. In that attack, a suicide bomber hit a high-profile congregation, wiping out the Sunni Tehreek's top leadership.[28] It was later discovered that Lashkar-e-Jhangvi was involved in the act.[29]

Losing the Center

OVER THE LAST THREE DECADES, BARELVISM AS A SCHOOL OF THOUGHT HAS ALSO become increasingly sidelined religiously and politically, just as the Deobandi and Ahl-e-Hadith schools have been strengthened. Although exact figures are unknown, the Barelvis are still considered to be the largest Islamic sect in Pakistan, and the country as a whole has undergone a broad-based religious revival, with the overall number of *madrassah*s from all sects and sub-sects increasing dramatically. Despite this, the total number of Barelvi madrassahs today stands second after Deobandi madrassahs. Dr. Tariq Rahman, a noted Pakistani scholar of education, calculates that with 7000 madrassahs in 2002 against 1779 in 1988, the number of Deobandi madrassahs has increased by 294 percent. Barelvi madrassahs, by contrast, saw only a 121 percent increase during the same period, with 717 madrassahs in 1988 and 1585 in 2002. In the view of Barelvis, these numbers reveal an undeniable reality: the struggle between Deobandism and Barelvism has intensified—and the trends suggest Barelvis are losing.

A number of factors account for the strengthening of Deobandi and other puritanical schools relative to the Barelvis over the past decades. In the 1980s, General Zia ul-Haq's domestic Islamization policies and participation in the anti-Soviet Afghan Jihad found enormous political support in movements and madrassahs connected to the Deobandi school of thought as well as the Jamaat-e-Islami.[30] Some of these schools also turned out committed militants, which the state has since used to conduct proxy wars, principally in Afghanistan and against "Hindu India." In the view of the ideologically-driven state, these puritan schools were a natural partner, as they were exclusive and selective in their identification of allies and adversaries, contrary to the Sufi-leaning Barelvis who were more inclusive and eclectic, and as a group eschewed political jihadism. (However, it should be kept in mind that Barelvis, too, have participated in the Kashmir insurgency, albeit on a much smaller scale than Deobandis.) Moreover, external assistance from Saudi Arabia and the Gulf States has also fed the growth of puritanical Islam within Pakistan—and especially the growth of the Ahl-e-Hadith, which has attracted Arab benefactors because of its affinities with Wahhabism.

In a recent move that has outraged Barelvis, Sipah-e-Sahaba Pakistan has started operating under the name of "Ahl-e-Sunnat wal Jamaat" (ASJ). The organization adopted the new name after it was banned for militant activities,[31] which included sectarian strikes on Shias and Barelvis. But the fact that the Deobandi ASJ has now claimed for itself the title of "Ahl-e-Sunnat" is especially scandalous to Barelvis, as they see themselves as the followers of true Islam and the Deobandis as deviant. According to Barelvi scholars, Deobandis have become so emboldened that the claim to represent "true Islam" is now being "stolen" by Deobandi ideologues who have "tried to impose their ideology on peaceful Pakistanis."[32]

Increasingly sidelined, and frequently targets of attack, Barelvis have as a whole reacted by becoming more political themselves, and in recent times they have organized to counter puritan ideologies that have been linked to rising sectarianism and terrorism. For these reasons, the present government led by the Pakistan People's Party (PPP) has actively courted Barelvism in an effort to rein in militancy and to acquire religious support for their counter-terrorism policies. The PPP government, for instance, has officially called for spreading the message of the Sufis—a policy meant to curtail the influence of puritan ideologies. In 2009, the Pakistani government set up an organization called the Sufi Advisory Council.[33] Among other things, the council was mandated to "propose steps to free religious thought from the rigidity imposed by some *ulema*."[34]

Barelvis, too, have organized new groups to counter puritan and militant ideologies. In 2009, several Barelvi groups established a new umbrella organization known as the Sunni Ittehad Council; its declared agenda is to tackle extremist ideology. The council, which was originally formed as an alliance of eight Barelvi organizations but is now reported to have twenty organizations,[35] has received a great deal of media attention for their loud and conspicuous messages designed to show how the mainstream *ulemas* support state-led counterterrorism operations. Indeed, the council has even called on Islamabad to speed up military operations in Pakistan's tribal areas against Deoband-inspired radical movements like the Taliban.[36]

On some levels, it seems natural for Barelvis to cooperate with the PPP government to combat what they have both denounced as the "Talibanization" of Pakistani society. Both PPP and Barelvis have been hit hard by militant Deobandi Islamists. Barelvis have been attacked for their religious beliefs and practices, whereas PPP politicians such as Benazir Bhutto have been assassinated for their progressive principles. Moreover, both the PPP and Barelvis have suffered from the country's tainted alliance between "mosque and military."[37] The PPP, for example, is quick to remind that their first government was subverted by General Zia ul-Haq, whose military regime favored puritan religious groups that later became engaged in sectarian and other terrorist activities.[38] Above all, the PPP has a large constituency in the rural areas of Sindh and the southern region of Punjab—both areas where Barelvism is the most common form of Islam. The present prime minister, Yusuf Raza Gillani, hails from southern Punjab and is respected as a descendant of a saint, and the very tombs of the Bhutto family in Sindh are visited by locals who seek spiritual solace—a practice common in rural parts of the subcontinent.[39]

Despite these ties and their common opponents, however, it would be a mistake to conclude that the Barelvis and PPP are seamlessly aligned in the struggle against all kinds of religiously-motivated extremism. The PPP, after all, is a progressive political party, whereas Barelvism is a religious movement. Their principles and agendas are different—and sometimes at odds. What matters most for the PPP as the ruling political party is retaining a numerical majority in the legislature. For this reason, the party has had to court the leading political force of the Deobandi school of thought, Jamaat Ulema Islam (JUI). The Barelvis' primary interest is in securing and propagating their religious teachings through *dawa*. As such, the numerous political parties and movements representing Barelvi populations may or may not align with the PPP, depending on the national and local context.

The limitations of the PPP-Barelvi partnership revealed themselves clearly in the national religious and political debate that unfolded in late 2010 when some PPP politicians including Governor Taseer proposed to re-examine the country's blasphemy laws. Barelvi organizations reacted by staging mass protests against the politician's proposals. Indeed, the same Sunni Ittehad Council created in 2009 by Barelvi scholars to "tackle Islamist militancy" was at the forefront of the protests against Governor Taseer, and the council threatened the state with "anarchy" should Aasia Bibi (the Christian woman sentenced to hang for speaking "ill" of the Prophet Muhammad) be pardoned of her crimes.[40] After Governor Taseer was killed, the council clearly lauded the assassin, with a spokesperson asserting "Don't associate Mumtaz with any terrorist group. He is a true lover of the Holy Prophet (pbuh)."[41] Needless to say, the Barelvi-PPP partnership against extremism has only further deteriorated since.

Securing the Prophet's Honor

WHAT DISTINGUISHES BARELVISM MOST VISIBLY FROM OTHER ISLAMIC SCHOOLS IN South Asia is the central importance it attaches to the veneration of the Prophet Muhammad. Unlike the Deobandis who are best known for their austerity, Barelvi religious practice is colorful and folksy, and it also reflects a great degree of variation at the local level. The festive rituals that Barelvis routinely partake in include the celebration of the birth of the Prophet; commemoration of saints (*walis*) at death anniversaries (*urs*); offering prayers at shrines constructed for the blessing of saints (a common Barelvi practice that is often simplistically described as "shrine worship"); as well as recitation of poems in honor of the Prophet Muhammad (*naat*). From the Deobandi and Ahl-e-Hadith perspectives, many of these common Barelvi practices—including, perhaps most notably, those associated with the Sufi belief in intercession through saints—are blatantly heretical.

Since Ahmed Raza's time, Barelvis have attached enormous significance to the veneration of the Prophet Muhammad, and this constitutes one of the sharpest areas of divergence between Barelvism and the puritan schools of thought. Barelvis regard their practices as reflecting their sincere and intense devotion to the Prophet Muhammad. They claim that the Deobandis and members of Ahl-e-Hadith do not show the full respect due to the sanctity of the Last Prophet. (Since Ahmed Raza's time, Barelvis have commonly described these puritan schools derisively as "Najdi,"[42] referring to Najd, the central region in modern-day Saudi Arabia where Wahhabi thought originated and which remains a bastion of reactionary Islam.)

The differences in the outward practices of these South Asian schools are rooted in their divergent doctrines. Barelvis, for instance, follow an esoteric understanding of Islam, and they believe that the Prophet Muhammad is light (*noor*). Deobandis, by contrast, believe that the Prophet Muhammad was merely human (*bashar*). Further, while Barelvis consider the Prophet to be present in this world at all times (*Hazir au Nazir*), Deobandis believe that he, a mortal, has passed away. Some Barelvis describe their devotion to Prophet Muhammad as so powerful that it harks back to an earlier era before Islam was revealed. This love is displayed in the Barelvi belief that Muhammad's creation "preceded that of Adam and the world in general."[43] For the Deobandis, however, any suggestion that the Prophet is more than human elevates his role to divinity, and thereby corrupts the monotheistic spirit of Islam.

On the basis of their beliefs, Barelvis commonly claim to derive deep spiritual satisfaction through the offering of prayers at shrines or by frequently reciting the Prophet's name in tandem after prayers. (Mumtaz Qadri himself was known for his passionate recitations of *naat*, or poems honoring the Prophet.) These physical acts of showing reverence for the Prophet and his followers are so integral to Barelvi understanding of Islam that they form the basis of the Barelvi claim to "Sunniat"—or that it is the Barelvis, and not the Deobandis, who are following true Islam as it was revealed and meant by God to be practiced.[44]

In the Barelvi view, a true Muslim is an "*Ashiq-e-Rasool*," or a "Lover of the Prophet," and it is this language of love, combined with the Barelvism's deeply Sufi messages on spiritual and social harmony, that largely accounts for the popular perception of Barelvi Islam as a moderate and peaceful teaching. At the same time, however, Barelvis also described Qadri's murder of Governor Taseer as the act of an *ashiq*—or of a devotee expressing his veneration to the Loved One. Moreover, the showering of flower petals on Qadri and the gifts sent to him on Valentine's Day are best understood as popular expressions of adoration and respect for a person who went to extreme lengths to show his devotion to the Prophet. As one of the assassin's admirers said, "We love Qadri because he loves the Holy Prophet (PBUH)!"[45]

With love and devotion to the Prophet Muhammad a central part of their faith, Barelvis commonly see themselves as religiously obligated to protect the sanctity of the Prophet. This includes showing no compromise toward all who might dishonor or blaspheme the Prophet. In 2006, for instance, the caricatures of the Prophet Muhammad published by the Danish newspaper *Jyllands Posten* outraged many Muslims and led to protests in many countries. Barelvis were among the most prominent groups in South Asia to voice their condemnation.

The Barelvis' deep-seated sense of obligation to defend the Prophet has from time to time led to zealous, even violent behavior. One underreported incident in 2008 involved a young Pakistani immigrant in Germany named Amir Cheema who attempted to murder the German publisher of the *Jyllands Posten* cartoons. Cheema was arrested, put behind bars, and he died in prison (reportedly from suicide, although some in Pakistan dispute this.) Since then, Cheema has been eulogized as a hero in Barelvi lore. Barelvi scholars of his native town in Punjab claim that Cheema was an Ahl-e-Sunnat—a true follower of the Prophet.[46] Before Cheema, Barelvi tradition similarly praised a line of heroes, including Ghazi Ilm Din Shaheed, who was convicted of murdering the Hindu publisher of a book that Muslims saw as libelous toward the Prophet in 1929 Lahore, which was then in British-occupied India. Today, many of the Barelvi websites that have been created to honor Mumtaz Qadri link his story with the heroic stories of Cheema and Ghazi Ilm Din Shaheed.[47]

Barelvism's devotion to the Prophet also helps to explain the ways in which Barelvis treat Muslim minorities, including Shiis and the Ahmadis. The Shiites, like the Barelvis, follow an esoteric Islamic teaching that is devoted to the Prophet, and the two groups share many rituals in common. Barelvis have also frequently combined with Shiites against their common foes, especially Deobandis and Ahl-e-Hadith. The Ahmadis, on the other hand, are a minority Muslim sect who, in the Barelvi view, do not accept the orthodox Sunni teaching that Muhammad was the last prophet and, therefore, are guilty of violating the Prophet's sanctity. Since Ahmed Raza's time, Barelvi scholars have thus categorically rejected Ahmadis as an heretical, un-Islamic movement, and the Barelvis have notoriously emerged as some of the most strident opponents of the Ahmadis in South Asia.

The Barelvi rejection of the Ahmadi beliefs has sometimes led to hostility and violence. Most famously, in 1953 massive riots erupted across the Punjab, and especially in Lahore, when members of several religious political groups—including the Barelvi organization Jamaat Ulema Pakistan, as well as Deobandis and activists from the Jamaat-e-Islami—took to the streets to demand that the government officially declare Ahmadis as non-Muslim. Barelvi leaders like Maulana Abdus Sattar Niazi were among the leaders of the mob, which demanded the removal of all Ahmadis from government posts (including the foreign minister.) The frenzied crowd was ultimately subdued only after the army managed to establish control in Lahore, leading to Pakistan's first taste of direct military involvement in civil affairs.

From time to time, Barelvis have managed to forge common ground with Deobandis against the Ahmadis—despite the fact that Deobandis and Barelvis also see each other as guilty of heresy. In 1974, for example, a joint platform known as the Tehreek-e-Khatm-e-Nabuwat, or the Movement for the Finality of Prophet, was created to launch a new campaign for rejecting the Ahmadis and restoring the sanctity of the Prophet Muhammad. That platform involved both Barelvi and Deobandi religious groups and, combined, they were able to exert enormous political pressure on the prime minister, Zulfiqar Ali Bhutto. The Pakistani government ultimately caved to this pressure, and in 1974 passed a constitutional amendment that officially declared Ahmadis as non-Muslims.

While Barelvi Islam has a reputation for being politically quietist, this is not entirely accurate, since Barelvis have historically been involved in pressuring the state to implement Islamic policies across the country. In 1977, for example, a nine-party coalition that included a large Barelvi contingent was organized to protest the government, which was then led by the Pakistan People's Party. Known as the Pakistan National Alliance (PNA), the coalition consisted of a variety of religious groups as well as a secular nationalist party. The PNA competed in the 1977 elections against Bhutto's PPP, and subsequently alleged that elections had been rigged. Perhaps the most remarkable, though not adequately studied, feature of this episode was the fact that the PNA coalition identified itself as the "Tehreek-e-Nizam-e-Mustafa," or the "Movement for the Establishment of Muhammad's Model." The movement's agenda was to replace the ruling PPP government with what it described as the "Model of Muhammad," which was a reference to the ideals of the Prophet's system of governance.[48] Prime Minister Bhutto again caved to this public pressure, and in hopes of reversing his political misfortunes, imposed bans on alcohol, horse racing, and night clubs and bars, and officially changed the weekly holiday from Sunday to Friday.

More recently, in 2002, in the wake of the U.S.-led NATO invasion of Afghanistan, a political alliance that included the Barelvi JUP party was created called the Muttahida Majlis Amal, or the United Council of Action (MMA). A central plank in the alliance's political agenda was opposing the NATO war in Afghanistan. The alliance additionally aimed to implement an Islamic system of governance, and it was able to introduce some reforms between 2002 and 2007, during its rule in the border province of Khyber Pakhtunkhwa (formerly known as North-West Frontier Province). The Barelvi JUP was only a minor partner in the MMA alliance; in fact, most of the seats were bagged by Jamaat-e-Islami and Jamaat Ulema Islam candidates.

The fact that Barelvis have from time to time cooperated with Deobandis (and also secular nationalists) for political reward or to counter a common enemy has become a subject of ongoing contention within the Barelvi school of thought. Some scholars have argued, after all, that cooperating with deviants like Deobandis diminishes the Barelvi claim to Sunniat, and therefore should be avoided at all costs. However, leading Barelvi scholars such as Dr. Tahir ul-Qadri have also rationalized the Barelvi cooperation with the Deobandis. In one of his speeches, he tried to persuade other Barelvis that despite the perception that a movement led by one apostate (such as the Deobandis) against another apostate (like the Ahmadis) may lessen the Sunniat (the Living the Way of the Prophet) among those who participate in the movement, such an alliance can serve a greater public or Islamic interest.[49]

The debate over whether Barelvis should cooperate with other schools of thought has itself become a source of division within the Barelvi movement. One especially controversial personality was Ahmed Shah Noorani, a scholar of great prestige and influence who died in 2003. A skilled political leader, he was a key Barelvi figure in all of the popular Barelvi movements—from the 1953 anti-Ahmadi riots to the 1974 and 1977 demonstrations against the PPP government. In 2002, Ahmed Shah was also elected president of MMA. For his activism and associations with non-Barelvi schools of thought, he was often accused by fellow Barelvis of being "*Qatil-e-Ahl-e-Sunnat*" (Killer of Ahl-e-Sunnat). However, Ahmed Shah also enjoys respect among some Barelvis because of his political activism and leadership of the Jamaat Ulema Pakistan during his lifetime.

Since Ahmed Shah's death, Barelvi political activists have been struggling to unite; the JUP itself was splintered into numerous factions. In the view of some Barelvis, the Sunni Ittehad Council was created in an effort to reunite Barelvis around a new common social and political agenda.[50] The council is in fact in the process of transforming itself into a political force and planning to compete in the next election.[51]

Shedding Quietism

PAKISTAN'S SECTARIAN STRIFE, GROWING INSECURITY, AND THE FEELING AMONG Barelvis that their communities are under siege have all contributed in recent years to the emergence of new forms of Barelvi activism and communalist assertion. It is within this context that we are best able to understand the widespread support in the Barelvi community for Mumtaz Qadri, as well as the increasing Barelvi hostility toward Deobandi militancy.

Conventionally, the Barelvi veneration for the Prophet Muhammad has formed the basis of the school's diehard support for Pakistan's blasphemy law. The blasphemy law, even though it purports to criminalize blaspheming against all religions, is commonly referred to in Urdu as "Tahafuz-e-Namoos Risalat Act," which means "Protection of the Sanctity of the Prophet Act." This is especially noteworthy from the Barelvi perspective, since the law explicitly concerns the Prophet and sanctity. Barelvis in particular have rallied in support of one specific clause in the law known as 295-C, which was added in 1986 by an act of parliament and meant to uphold respect for the Prophet.[52] For the Barelvis, 295-C has become a rallying point for asserting their communalist identity and claims to being the true followers of Islam.

In 2000, for example, General Musharraf's government announced that it would be reviewing the blasphemy laws.[53] This inflamed Barelvi groups, who poured into Pakistan's streets to protest against the government. In response, Musharraf's government backed off from amending the law. The religious groups later organized into a pro-blasphemy law movement known as the Tehreek-e-Namoos Risalat Muhammadi, or the Movement for the Preservation of the Sanctity of the Prophet Muhammad.[54] (Incidentally, the "brain behind the movement," Mufti Sarfraz Naeemi, a Barelvi scholar, was killed in 2009 in a suicide bomb attack a few days after his denouncement of terrorism.[55] He was one of the first Barelvi scholars to have issued a fatwa against suicide bombing in 2005.)[56]

While both Deobandi and Barelvi scholars have championed the blasphemy law, they have done so for different reasons—and this difference, too, has become a source of increasing tension between the schools over who represents "true Islam." The Barelvi support for the law stems from their veneration of the Prophet and their sense of obligation to protect his sanctity. Deobandis, for their part, reject this Barelvi devotion to the Prophet as heretical (claiming it is an act of *shirk*, polytheism). These differences have expressed themselves through the divergent reactions of the two Islamic schools to Taseer's assassination. For example, Allama Tahir Ashrafi, the Chairman of the Pakistan Ulema Council, a Deobandi organization, distanced the Deobandi school from Mumtaz Qadri, commenting that "sentiments [i.e., the veneration of Muhammad] were being exploited" against Taseer.[57] (Incidentally, in 2007, this same Deobandi scholar ruled that Muslims should honor Osama bin Laden in reaction to the British government's granting of knighthood to Salman Rushdie.)[58]

In an apparent tit-for-tat reaction to sectarian strikes and increasing marginalization, Barelvi communities around Pakistan have begun to shed their politically quietest ways and to assert themselves by organizing mass religious processions, organizing new groups, and staging rallies. While the majority of these public gatherings have not been outwardly militant (the tenor at the rallies in defense of the blasphemy law and Mumtaz Qadri were a clear exception to this), they are increasing in frequency and scale, and they are clearly meant as displays of Barelvi strength and unity against their ideological rivals.

This Barelvi activism has brought new pressures to bear on the state—and all at a time when the state's own capacity to cope with sectarianism and secure the country has been greatly depleted. In July 2010, for example, a famous shrine in Lahore known as Data Darbar was bombed. Frustrated by the government's failure to stop attacks even inside the provincial capital, Barelvi scholars met with the Punjab Chief Minister and publicly criticized top government officials, claiming they sympathized with the Deobandis and were linked with the Taliban.[59] Later, in a public gathering against suicide bombing in August 2010, the chief of the Sunni Ittehad Council Fazl-e-Karim, declared that the Punjab Government will come to know "how powerful"[60] the Barelvis are, and that they will "no longer remain silent."[61]

Meanwhile, Deobandi scholars have accused the same Punjab government of favoring the Barelvis. Only two weeks after the Darbar attack, Deobandi activists responded to the Barelvi criticisms by stating that the Sunni Ittehad Council "is conspiring to cause Deobandi-Barelvi riots." They further stated that the *Khadm-e-Ala* (the Punjab Chief Minister; literally "the Chief Servant" of the people) seems to be *Khadm-i-Barelvi* ("Servant of the Barelvis"), and they warned that "if the Punjab government does not stop patronizing (the Barelvis), a campaign will be launched to make the next elections a contest between Deobandi and Barelvi schools of thought."[62]

Due in part to their lack of confidence in the state to provide security, Barelvis have also begun to organize their communities to defend against sectarian groups. One of the most notable of these organizations is the Sunni Tehreek, which has engaged in frequent clashes with Deobandi activists since it was created in the early 1990s. A 2007 International Crisis Group report described the Sunni Tehreek as a "Barelvi militant group" that was created to "defend Barelvi mosques and interests against take-overs and intimidation by Deobandi groups."[63]

The Sunni Tehreek disputes the characterization that it is a "militant" movement, and it has repeatedly claimed it is deliberately slandered when people accuse it of engaging in violence. According to one Barelvi, the Sunni Tehreek is not a "militant" movement like the groups associated with Deobandis or Ahl-e-Hadith, but a "defensive" organization created to actively repel attacks on the Barelvi community and their places of worship.[64]

However Sunni Tehreek is characterized now or in the future, it cannot be denied that it represents a new kind of Barelvi organization whose importance within Pakistani political life is also growing. Before the Sunni Tehreek's emergence in the mid-1990s, according to the International Crisis Group, "no prominent Barelvi organization had indulged in organized sectarian violence."[65] In 2002, the International Crisis Group described the Sunni Tehreek as representing only a "miniscule fringe" of the Barelvi community in Karachi.[66] Yet the rapid growth of Sunni Tehreek and similar community activist organizations since then has been undeniable. This growth has been spurred on by rising sectarianism and the Barelvi population's felt need for enhanced security and for asserting their communal identity. The Sunni Tehreek has since emerged as a major political force—and not only in Karachi, but nationally. In a recent sign of the organization's growing importance and influence, the Prime Minister of Pakistan recently called upon Sunni Tehreek to participate in an All-Parties Conference whose purpose was to think through Pakistan's approach to deteriorating relations with the United States.

Conclusion

THE OUTPOURING OF BARELVI SUPPORT FOR MUMTAZ QADRI'S MURDER OF GOVERNOR Salman Taseer has deeply upset many commonly held assumptions about Barelvi moderation and also about the sources of religious extremism in Pakistan. When it was announced on October 1, 2011 that Mumtaz Qadri would be executed for his crimes, a new wave of mass demonstrations involving Barelvi groups took hold across the country. These riots are taking place against the backdrop of a larger revival of Barelvi activism and communalist assertion that has become an undeniable force in Pakistan's religious politics.

There have been additional indications of new forms of Barelvi militancy in recent months. In September 2011, for instance, it was reported that the Pakistani military had decided to curtail the proselytizing activities of the Dawat-e-Islami, out of fear that the Barelvi organization was penetrating the ranks, seeking to radicalize soldiers.[67] (Mumtaz Qadri, it must be recalled, was a member of Dawat-e-Islami.) Also in September 2011, amidst rumors that the U.S. might invade Pakistan to disrupt jihadist networks along the country's Afghan border, the Barelvi Sunni Ittehad Council issued a fatwa declaring jihad against the U.S. to be obligatory should it encroach upon Pakistani soil.[68] The fatwa additionally urged the Pakistan government to abandon Pakistan's role as a front-line ally in the struggle against the Taliban and al-Qaeda, to realign the country geopoliti-cally, and to prepare the country as a whole for a jihad in the way of God.

Importantly, not all Barelvi scholars and organizations have embraced this extremist agenda, and some have actively resisted it. For example, the religious scholar Tahrir ul-Qadri, one of Pakistan's most outspoken critics of Islamic terrorism, has also emerged as one of the few Barelvi scholars to have categorically condemned Mumtaz Qadri's mur-der Salman Taseer.[69] Tahrir ul-Qadri has additionally called for religious moderation as well as new efforts to rein in sectarianism strife between different Islamic sects. Despite this, however, Tahrir ul-Qadri and his followers are frequently criticized by Barelvi activists for not being in touch with the concerns of ordinary Barelvis. Revealingly, his organization, Minahaj-ul-Quran, is also criticized for not being in line with mainstream Barelvi thought, nor is it a member of the Sunni Ittehad Council.

Taken as a whole, the events surrounding the murder of Governor Taseer provide a number of cautionary lessons for the struggle with Islamist militancy. It has often been proposed that states should actively support and ally with Islamic schools of thought whose ideas run counter to and can compete with extremist ideologies. For example, a number of policy studies, including several issued by Western think tanks, have sug-gested partnering with and supporting Sufi movements in an effort to curtail the influ-ence of radical Deobandi and Salafist-inspired militancy in South Asia and elsewhere.[70] While engaging non-violent religious groups is always a sound policy, the case of Pak-istan has shown the limitations of certain strategies that involve using "moderate Islam" against "radical Islam"—as well as its potential to backfire.

The advocates of state support for one religious group against another commonly assume that states will dramatically enhance their ability to curtail the influence of religiously-based radical movements if they have the support of religious scholars. Such proposals frequently also link militant radicalism to a specific ideological current, and thus they simplistically equate violence and sectarianism with a particular ideology. While it is true that certain ideological currents today are more prone to violence than others, the Barelvi reaction to the murder of Governor Taseer demonstrates that even purportedly moderate religious ideologies may themselves be exploited and utilized to promote extremist and violent agendas.

Moreover, the proponents of providing state support to some religious groups to counter the influence of other groups frequently neglect the fundamental and often conflicting interests that naturally exist between the modern state and religious groups. They frequently forget, for example, how the Pakistani state's past support of specific Islamic groups to advance the state's own political agendas has inadvertently encouraged the growth of new religious and political dynamics, including the intensification of the now more than a century old sectarian struggle between Deobandis and Barelvis. In light of this, it is worth asking the question: if the Pakistani state were to seek to systematically support Barelvis against Deobandis, how might it affect the future evolution of sectarianism and religious politics in the country as a whole?

In the wake of the 1953 riots against Ahmadi Muslims, Pakistan's government established a commission to investigate the causes of religious violence in society.[71] The commission's final report looked, among other things, at the nature of sectarianism, and described how the relentless efforts of Muslim groups to declare other Muslim groups as "un-Islamic" can destroy any possibility for a healthy and normal political life:

> The net result of all this is that neither Shias nor Sunnis nor Deobandis nor Ahl-i-Hadith nor Barelvis are Muslims and any change from one view to the other must be accompanied in an Islamic State with the penalty of death if the Government of the State is in the hands of the party which considers the other party to be *kafirs*. And it does not require much imagination to judge of the consequences of this doctrine when it is remembered that no two *ulama* have agreed before us as to the definition of a Muslim. If the constituents of each of the definitions given by the *ulama* are given effect to, and subjected to the rule of 'combination and permutation' and the form of charge in the Inquisition's sentence on Galileo is adopted *mutatis mutandis* as a model, the grounds on which a person may be indicted for apostasy will be too numerous to count.[72]

These observations are perhaps even more relevant today than they were sixty years ago, at a time when Pakistan struggles to find a new basis for a national politics beyond Islamic ideology. This remains the singular challenge for Pakistan.

NOTES

1. "Mumtaz Qadri admits killing Governor Salman Taseer," *BBC News,* January 10, 2011, http://www.bbc.co.uk/news/world-south-asia-12149607.
2. The "Blasphemy Law" refers to a set of clauses of Pakistani law which were collectively introduced in the 1980s as part of General Zia ul-Haq's program of state-led Islamization. It must, however, be remembered that the first clause of the law—295-A of Pakistan Penal Code—was introduced by the British in 1927, and that the later clauses were added to this foundation. Because these laws were implemented under the military ruler, there has been an ongoing debate over their legal position.

    One of the many problems with the law is that it allows for a case to be filed against someone on the basis of them allegedly using "innuendos" and "insinuations" to desecrate religion. Moreover, critics argue that the law is frequently used to settle personal scores, while others point out that the law targets religious minorities. Furthermore, even when a charge of blasphemy is dropped or the accused person is allowed bail, the accused person often receives death threats and is sometimes the target of vigilante killings. For these and other reasons, even those who support the law in principle sometimes disagree with its misapplication.

3. Rob Crilly and Aoun Sahi, "Christian woman sentenced to death in Pakistan 'for blasphemy'," *The Telegraph,* November 9, 2010, http://www.telegraph.co.uk/news/religion/8120142/Christian-woman-sentenced-to-death-in-Pakistan-for-blasphemy.html.

4. "Pressure grows for pardon of Aasia bibi," *Dawn,* November 22, 2010, http://www.dawn.com/2010/11/22/pressure-grows-for-pardon-of-aasia-bibi.html.

5. Usman Manzoor, "Events that led to Taseer's murder," *The News,* January 06, 2011 http://www.thenews.com.pk/TodaysPrintDetail.aspx?ID=24207&Cat=2.

6. Babar Dogar, "Pakistan governor's suspected assassin hailed as hero," *The Washington Times,* January 5, 2011, http://www.washingtontimes.com/news/2011/jan/5/pakistani-governor-buried-under-tightened-security/.

7. Waqar Hamza, "Over 1,000 people like Mumtaz Qadri's fan pages on Facebook," *Pakistan Today,* http://www.pakistantoday.com.pk/2011/01/over-1000-people-like-mumtaz-qadris-fan-pages-on-facebook/.

8. "Valentine gifts for Mumtaz Qadri," *The Express Tribune,* February 14, 2011, http://tribune.com.pk/story/118594/valentine-gifts-for-mumtaz-qadri/.

9. The statement was released from the platform of Jamaat Ahl-e- Sunnat Pakistan (JASP), a Barelvi group; See: Salman Siddiqui, "Hardline Stance: Religious bloc condones murder," *The Express Tribune,* http://tribune.com.pk/story/99313/hardline-stance-religious-bloc-condones-murder/.

10. In a report complied for a leading Pakistani paper, JASP is termed as the "largest body of the Barelvi group" whose "directions are considered binding on every other organization." See: http://tribune.com.pk/story/99313/hardline-stance-religious-bloc-condones-murder/. The JASP calls itself a "religious organization representing the over whelming majority of Pakistan." See: http://jamateahlesunnat.org/.

11. "Top prayer leaders deny Taseer his rites," *Pakistan Today,* http://www.pakistantoday.com.pk/2011/01/top-prayer-leaders-deny-taseer-his-rites/.

12. "Journalist Recalls Father's Assassination In Pakistan," *NPR,* June 27, 2011, http://www.npr.org/2011/06/27/137441962/shehrbano-taseer-recalls-her-fathers-assassination.

13. In one of his sermons, Allama Syed Turab Qadri, a noted scholar, after distancing Qadri's act from any collective involvement, laid down the legal and religious mechanism that deals with someone who violates the sanctity of Islam—and associates it with the Governor's statement. http://www.alahazrat.net/askimam/content.php?id=1137.

14. Article 248 (3) of the 1973 Constitution of Islamic Republic of Pakistan states, "No process for the arrest or imprisonment of the President or a Governor shall issue from any court during his term of office." http://www.pakistani.org/pakistan/constitution/part12.ch4.html.

15. Interview with a Barelvi activist (anonymity requested); moreover, Qadri's counsel also tried to prove that Qadri took up arms against Governor because of his "sudden provocation." See: "Defence tries to prove Qadri acted on 'sudden provocation'," *The Express Tribune,* July 24, 2011, http://tribune.com.pk/story/216265/defence-tries-to-prove-qadri-acted-on-sudden-provocation/.

16. "ST warns govt of besieging parliament if Qadri given death," *Daily Times,* January 10, 2011, http://www.dailytimes.com.pk/default.asp?page=2011\01\10\story_10-1-2011_pg7_2.

17. "Taseer assassination: Self-confessed killer insists he was 'not influenced'," *The Express Tribune*, January 11, 2011,

    http://tribune.com.pk/story/102103/taseer-assassination-self-confessed-killer-insists-he-was-not-influenced/.

18. The video of the sermon can be accessed here:

    http://www.shababeislami.com/mumtaz%20Qadri.html.

19. Karin Brulliard, "In Pakistan, even anti-violence Islamic sect lauds assassination of liberal governor," *Washington Post*, January 29, 2011,

    http://www.washingtonpost.com/wp-dyn/content/article/2011/01/29/AR2011012904706.html.

20. One scholar, for instance, argues that they are not different but instead follow the belief in the way of the saints. See: Saqib Akbar (ed.), *Pakistan Kay Deeni Masalik*, (*Pakistan's Muslim Creeds*), Al-Baseera, December 2010, pg. 13.

21. For his pioneering role, Ahmed Shah Barelvi is often known as "*Ala Hazrat*" and "*Imam ahl-e-Sunnat*" (*Imam* of the Ahl-e-Sunnat).

22. As the movement's name suggests, Ahl-e-Hadith members adhere only to the Quran and the *Hadiths* and, unlike Deobandis and Barelvis, do not follow any tradition of jurisprudence (*taqlid*). For their puritan observation, they have been called the "Wahhabis of South Asia," a reference to the strict interpretation followed in Saudi Arabia. The pioneers of Ahl-e-Hadith wrote in and were criticized in the earlier nineteenth century—more than half a century before the life of Ahmed Raza Khan. See for example the critique of Shah Ismail Shaheed's "*Taqwatul Iman*" (Strengthening of Faith); see: Saqib Akbar (ed.), *Pakistan Kay Deeni Masalik* (*Pakistan's Muslim Creeds*), Al-Baseera, December 2010, pg. 11.

23. Usha Sanyal, 108.

24. Interview with a Barelvi activist (anonymity requested).

25. Interview with a Barelvi activist (anonymity requested). For instance, the interviewee said that the original manifesto of SSP was "kafir kafir, Barelvi kafir" which was changed against "Shia only later." Special reference was made to Manazira-e-Jhang—which took place years before SSP was formally formed.

26. See: http://terrorismwatch.com.pk/images/Timeline%20Of%20attacks%20on%20Shrines%20In%20Pakistan.pdf.

27. Muhammad Faisal Ali, "Suicide bomber kills anti-Taliban cleric Allama Naeemi," *Dawn*, June 13, 2009, http://archives.dawn.com/archives/34664.

28. "Bomb carnage at Karachi prayers," *BBC News*, April 11, 2006,

    http://news.bbc.co.uk/2/hi/south_asia/4900402.stm.

29. "Lashkar-e-Jhangvi Suicide Bomber Behind 2006 Nishtar Park Killing," *Dawn*, June 15, 2007,

    http://watandost.blogspot.com/2007/06/lashkar-e-jhangvi-suicide-bomber-behind.html.

30. The Deobandi school of thought, for instance, remains the dominant school of thought in the western region of Pakistan, including tribal areas.

31. Syed Shoaib Hasan, "Pakistan 'extremist' is shot dead," *BBC News*, August 17, 2009,

    http://news.bbc.co.uk/2/hi/8205158.stm.

32. Mufti Gulzar Naeema argues that by attaching the whole movement as "Barelvi" only, a banned group has taken the name. Saqib Akbar (ed.), *Pakistan Kay Deeni Masalik* (*Pakistan's Muslim Creeds*), Al-Baseera, December 2010, pg. 13.

33. "Sufi Advisory Council constituted," *Daily Times*, June 8, 2009,

    http://www.dailytimes.com.pk/default.asp?page=2009\06\08\story_8-6-2009_pg7_32.

34. The official notification along with terms of reference can be accessed at the Ministry of Religious Affairs' website:

http://202.83.164.27/wps/portal/Morazu/!ut/p/c0/04_SB8K8xLLM9MSSzPy8xBz9CP0os_hQN68AZ3dnI wML82BTAyNXTz9jE0NfQwNfA_2CbEdFAA2MC_Y!/?WCM_GLOBAL_CONTEXT=/wps/wcm/connect/ MorazuCL/ministry/highlights/reconstitution+of+the+sufi+advisory+council.
Even the founding chairman of the council condoned Taseer's assassination. See: Imtiaz Gul, "Pakistan's dangerous blasphemy laws claim the governor of Punjab," *Af-Pak Channel*, Foreign Policy (online), January 4, 2011,
http://afpak.foreignpolicy.com/posts/2011/01/04/pakistan_s_dangerous_blasphemy_laws_claim_the_ governor_of_punjab.

35. "Fatwa for Jihad against America Published," September 26, 2011, *The Nation*,
http://nation.com.pk/pakistan-news-newspaper-daily-english-online/Regional/Lahore/26-Sep-2011/Fatwa-for-Jihad-against-America.

36. Correspondent, "Eight parties form alliance against Talibanisation," *The News*, May 09, 2009,
http://www.thenews.com.pk/TodaysPrintDetail.aspx?ID=22032&Cat=13&dt=5/10/2009.

37. For a detailed overview, read Husain Haqqani, "Pakistan: Beyond Mosque and Military." Carnegie Endowment for International Peace, 2005.

38. It is, however, important to remember that PPP was opposed by Jamiat Ulema Pakistan, a Barelvi political party; the orgnization's religious manifesto is counted as one of the domestic reasons behind Zia's Islamization immediately upon his overthrow of the government.

39. These tombs mark the grave of Zulfiqar Ali Bhutto, who was hanged after Zia-ul-Haq overthrew his government, and Benazir Bhutto, who was killed in 2007.

40. "Sunni Ittehad Council warns of 'anarchy' if Aasia pardoned," *The Express Tribune*, November 26, 2010,
http://tribune.com.pk/story/82149/sunni-ittehad-council-warns-of-anarchy-if-aasia-pardoned/.

41. Rana Tanveer, "Taseer murder: Sunni Ittehad warns against protests," *The Express Tribune*, January 10, 2011, http://tribune.com.pk/story/101580/taseer-murder-sunni-ittehad-warns-against-protests/.

42. One Barelvi scholar narrates the genesis of Barelvi history referencing the inroads of "Najdi movement"; see: Saqib Akbar (ed.), *Pakistan Kay Deeni Masalik, Pakistan's Muslim Creeds)*, Al-Baseera, December 2010, pg. 12.

43. Usha Sanyal, *Ahmed Riza Khan Barelwi: In the Path of the Prophet*, Viva Books Private Limited, 2006, pg. 96.

44. This claim is clearly visible in the symbolism of many Barelvi groups. A few examples include: "Jamaat Ahl-e-Sunnat Pakistan" (JASP); Sunni Tehreek, a Barelvi outfit with stains of militant activities; the title *Ahl-e-Sunnat wal Jamaat*; Sunni Ittehad Council, an anti-terrorism platform supported by Barelvi-inspired groups; and even Madani TV, a Barelvi TV channel (the name refers to Medina, burial city of the Prophet).

45. "Valentine gifts for Mumtaz Qadri," *The Express Tribune*, February 14, 2011,
http://tribune.com.pk/story/118594/valentine-gifts-for-mumtaz-qadri/.

46. One cleric challenged his opponents, in a sermon, that if Cheema was of "your" faith, how come Cheema's *chehlum* (procession on the 40th day of a death) be held, how come people visit his shrine, etc. *See:* http://www.youtube.com/watch?v=0RGhEXtEQ1Y.

47. Examples include: http://www.mumtazqadri.info.

48. It cannot be said for sure what Barelvis and other alliance members meant by this term. The slogan has stuck with Barelvi political movements since, and is used to show their devotion to the Prophet. For example, Dr. Tahrir ul-Qadri used the term as the title of his first book (1978). See:
http://www.irfan-ul-quran.com/quran/english/tid/41/.

49. "Tahreek-e-Khatam Nabuwat under Deobandi Leadership? Where was your Sunniat?," http://www.youtube.com/watch?v=Smzfq8obf0g (Last accessed July 4, 2010).

50. Interview with a Barelvi activist (anonymity requested).

51. However, SIC's decision to actively participate in the political process is by itself debated within the SIC. See: Karamat Bhatty, "OF RELIGION AND POLITICS – Infighting over SIC's involvement in politics," April 14, 2011, *Pakistan Today*, http://www.pakistantoday.com.pk/2011/04/of-religion-and-politics-infighting-over-sics-involvement-in-politics/.

52. The full clause reads, "Whoever by words, either spoken or written, or by visible representation or by any imputation, innuendo, or insinuation, directly or indirectly, defiles the sacred name of the Holy Prophet Muhammad (peace be upon him) shall be punished with death, or imprisonment for life, and shall also be liable to fine."
See: http://www.pakistani.org/pakistan/legislation/1860/actXLVof1860.html.

53. "Owen Bennett-Jones, Pakistan's blasphemy law U-turn," *BBC World*, 17 May, 2000, http://news.bbc.co.uk/2/hi/south_asia/751803.stm.

54. Aoun Sahi, "The price of defiance," *The News on Sunday*, June 21, 2009, http://jang.com.pk/thenews/jun2009-weekly/nos-21-06-2009/dia.htm.

55. IBID.

56. IBID.

57. "Sentiments were exploited against Salmaan Taseer: Ashrafi," *Daily Times*, January 9, 2011 http://www.dailytimes.com.pk/default.asp?page=2011%5C01%5C09%5Cstory_9-1-2011_pg7_18.

58. Duncan Campbell, "Bhutto condemns Rushdie attack," *The Guardian*, June 22, 2007, http://www.guardian.co.uk/uk/2007/jun/22/pakistan.religion.

59. M Ilyas Khan, "Pakistan clerics accuse Punjab leaders of Taliban link," *BBC News*, Islamabad, BBC World, 5 July 2010, http://www.bbc.co.uk/news/10511046.

60. News report, "Sunni clerics vow show of strength," *The Express Tribune*, August 8, 2010, http://tribune.com.pk/story/37108/sunni-clerics-vow-show-of-strength/.

61. News report, "SUI announces long march against terrorism," The News, August 09, 2010, http://www.thenews.com.pk/TodaysPrintDetail.aspx?ID=30622&Cat=13&dt=8/9/2010.

62. "Deoband elders' warning to Punjab govt," *Dawn*, July 14, 2010 http://archives.dawn.com/archives/151111.

63. Crisis Group Report, "Pakistan: Karachi's Madrasas and Violent Extremism," International *Crisis Group*, March 29, 2007, pg. 26, http://www.crisisgroup.org/~/media/Files/asia/southasia/pakistan/130_pakistan_karachi_s_madrasas_and_violent_extremism.ashx.

64. Interview with a Barelvi activist (anonymity requested).

65. Crisis Group Report, "Pakistan: Karachi's Madrasas and Violent Extremism," *International Crisis Group*, March 29, 2007, pg. 11, http://www.crisisgroup.org/~/media/Files/asia/southasia/pakistan/130_pakistan_karachi_s_madrasas_and_violent_extremism.ashx.

66. IBID, pg. 12.

67. Kamran Yousaf, "Dawat-e-Islami comes under military's radar," *The Express Tribune*, September 12, 2011, http://tribune.com.pk/story/250572/clamping-down-dawat-e-islami-comes-under-militarys-radar/.

68. This was published in Urdu newspapers; see also "Fatwa for Jihad against America," *Nation*, September 26, 2011,

http://nation.com.pk/pakistan-news-newspaper-daily-english-online/Regional/Lahore/26-Sep-2011/Fatwa-for-Jihad-against-America.

69. Watch "Dr Tahir Ul Qadri's Views about Salman Taseer and Gazi Mumtaz Qadri" at http://www.youtube.com/watch?v=Ufb5UfXTYUg.

70. See, for instance, RAND's recommendation of encouraging "Sufism": http://www.rand.org/pubs/monograph_reports/2005/MR1716.sum.pdf and Heritage Foundation's report on supporting pluralism: http://www.heritage.org/Research/Reports/2009/05/Reviving-Pakistans-Pluralist-Traditions-to-Fight-Extremism.

71. As discussed, in 1953, Lahore was engulfed in riots against Ahmadis, a minority sect; Barelvi activists and scholars participated in the protests. The demonstrations got out of control, the army was called in, and a Commission was formed to investigate the causes of riots.

72. "Report of the Court of Inquiry Constituted Under Punjab Act II of 1954 to Enquire Into the Punjab Disturbances of 1953," pg. 219, http://www.thepersecution.org/dl/report_1953.pdf.

The Extremist Reaction to the UK's Prevent Strategy

By Jack Barclay

THE EFFORTS OF THE BRITISH GOVERNMENT IN SUMMER 2011 TO RE-launch a controversial strategy to combat violent radicalization has prompted a furious response from the country's Islamist activists and groups. The updated strategy, known as "Prevent," promises a comprehensive approach to contesting extremist ideologies, supporting vulnerable individuals and communities susceptible to extremist messages, and working closely with a range of institutions such as schools, prisons, and charities to help them play an active part in addressing radicalization.

Prevent was first launched in 2007 as a component of the government's national counterterrorism strategy known as "CONTEST." Prevent's focus on violent Islamist radicalization was a reflection of the fact that al-Qaeda-inspired terrorism was—and still is —seen by government as the pre-eminent terrorist threat to the UK and its interests. Nevertheless, this focus quickly raised concerns among some of the UK's Muslim populations that they were going to be unfairly stigmatized as communities under suspicion. Some accused the government of using Prevent to spy on Muslim communities (which the government denies) while others criticized it for funding a range of broader, social cohesion projects that appeared to have little to do with counter-radicalization. The latest iteration of Prevent, government claims, addresses these shortcomings.

The re-launch of Prevent was met with open hostility by a variety of Muslim and Islamist groups in the UK, but especially from extremists who support the contemporary violent jihadist movement. These extremists see the Prevent strategy as a direct challenge to their declared mission of promoting a militant Islamist awakening, or *sahwah*, among British Muslim youth.

In some cases, the extremists have attempted to leverage pre-existing concerns about

Prevent among parts of the broader UK Muslim population. For instance, they have attempted to exploit suspicions that Prevent is a cover for domestic intelligence collection, despite repeated assertions to the contrary by government officials. They have also tried to stoke fears that the government is attempting to interfere in Muslims' free practice and propagation of their religion, and they promote the narrative that Prevent is an attempt to corrupt the Islamic identity of Muslim youth by actively spreading liberal and secular principles contrary to those of Islam.

Some of the individuals involved in protesting Prevent today are led by an activist movement that formerly belonged to the now disbanded group known as "Al-Muhajiroun," or "The Emigres." Although these activists see themselves as practicing and propagating their ideology in accordance with the tenets of the Salafi movement, other Salafi communities in the UK appear to regard them as too extreme, and often pejoratively refer to them as "*Takfiris*" or "*Khawarij.*"[1] The leaders of this extreme movement see Prevent as the key plank of an ideological offensive against British Muslims and Islam more generally, and they refer to this offensive as *al-ghazwat al-fikri*, or the "ideological raid." They view this offensive as a fundamental attack on the Islamic *Aqidah*—in other words, as an attempt by the government to spread a watered-down, pacifist "UK Islam" that would effectively divert Muslim youth from a correct understanding of their religion, including the obligation to implement Islam at societal and state levels and to defend by both word and deed the threats to their religion and their fellow Muslims.

The extremists clearly take the challenges posed by Prevent seriously. Their response to the government's strategy has been unprecedented in its focus and duration, and they have used innovative new tactics to frustrate the implementation of the strategy at the local level. This reaction has raised a number of questions about the current outlook of these Islamist extremists in the UK and their purpose. Why has Prevent generated such a furious backlash? Why do the extremists consider Prevent such a significant threat to Islam, and specifically to the identity of Muslim youth in Britain? Moreover, what do they believe is an appropriate response to what they describe as an infidel government's attempts to attack the religion of Muslims that reside in the UK? And what measures do these Islamists ultimately deem acceptable in this battle for the hearts and minds of their co-religionists?

The Ideological Raid

UK ISLAMISTS VIEW THE PREVENT STRATEGY AS A DIRECT THREAT TO WHAT THEY understand as their obligation to re-Islamize and mobilize British Muslim youth in defense of Islam, whether by non-violent activism or through violent jihad. The extremists have long been wary of Prevent and other perceived governmental attempts to interfere in their propagation of Islam. In 2010, a prominent Islamist known most commonly by his *kunya* (nickname), Abu Walid, delivered a lecture in which he characterized Prevent as part of an "ideological war" being waged against Islam by the British government.[2] In this lecture Abu Walid warned that many Muslims were oblivious to the government's agenda and its tactics, stating further that,

> Nowadays we see that there is an ongoing Crusade against Islam and Muslims. That battle is being fought on two fronts—the physical battle and the ideological battle.

> On the physical front we can see what is going on...but from the ideological side people are unaware...they are unaware of the ideological crusade against Islam and the Muslims whereby the kuffar want to try and change the *deen* [religion] from within. They talk about this reformation of Islam, a battle for hearts and minds. There is a battle for hearts and minds going on—his is not something which is being taken lightly by the *kuffar*.

Abu Walid then appeared to single out the Prevent strategy as an example of how the ideological offensive was being waged in the UK. He highlighted the hundreds of millions of dollars being spent by the government on counter-radicalization programs in Muslim communities, and said,

> They the *kuffar* will never stop fighting you until—what? Until they get Afghanistan? Until they get Iraq? Allah said they will never stop fighting you until they make you become *kaffir*. Until they make you turn back from your *deen* [religion].[3]

In another lecture this year entitled "Prevent Strategy" (and which was possibly recorded sometime between May and June), Abu Walid warned that unlike high-profile conflicts in countries such as Iraq and Afghanistan, where the enemy's intentions toward Muslims were obvious, Muslims in the UK were unaware of the government's attempts to spread secularism and divert the youth from developing a complete understanding of their religion:

> When someone comes into your house through the front door you know he's there. When he comes in through the back door you've no idea he's there...until he's stolen your TV... This attack through the back door is called *al-Ghazwat al-Fikri*—the ideological war. Most people do

not know this is going on. Nowadays they come with these initiatives like Prevent, counterterrorism schemes and scams...Peace TV, the Islam Channel, the GPU [Global Peace and Unity Conference]...they will seek to turn your back from your *deen* if they can.

Such narratives are UK-centric variations on a theme originally propagated by other English-speaking extremist ideologues such as Anwar al-Awlaki, the U.S.-Yemeni preacher killed in a U.S. air strike in Yemen in September 2011. Al-Awlaki warned Western Muslims against the threat presented by what he referred to as "RAND-Islam"[4]—a pacifist version of the religion that promotes secularism and Muslim integration into Western societies at the expense of fundamental Islamic obligations including belief and implementation of *tawhid* (monotheism), *al-Wala wal-Bara* (enjoining good and forbidding evil), and violent *jihad*.

This theme was subsequently explored by another leading Islamist activist, Anjem Choudhary (a.k.a. Abu Luqman), in a lecture entitled "The Role Of The Muslims" that appeared on an extremist web site in June 2011. Choudhary, who sometimes refers to himself as "the former UK Emir of Al-Muhajiroun," attacked fellow Muslims who compromised their religious practice in order to integrate into non-Muslim society. He complained that many Muslims living in the UK had become "stripped of their Islamic personality:"

> [They are] part-time Muslims. Muslim when it comes to the prayer; Muslim when it comes to the fasting; Muslim when it comes to the wife, the *halal* food, the circumcision, the burial site, the *masjid*.

> But when it comes to the struggle, to liberate our lands, when it comes to raise the banner of *Tawhid*, when it comes to shake the *Firaun* [Pharaoh] of our time, then we are just like the *kaafir*. Our ambition to be like the *kaafir*, to behave like the *kaafir*, to speak like the kaafir, dress like the *kaafir*, to die like the *kaafir*.

> Indeed the *nabi* [Prophet] *sallalahu walahi wa'salam* said I am worried for my own *al-Sahabah*...because there will come a time when there will be those, with the tongue of a Muslim but the heart of a *kaafir*.

Abdul Muhid, another prominent Islamist activist who is known as Abu Wala'a, delivered a Paltalk lecture in June 2011 entitled "Obstacles in the Dawa" in which he claimed that Prevent was not a counter-extremism program but instead an attempt to stop sincere young Muslims "from practicing Islam...from having any inclination towards

Sharia...[and from] preventing you from achieving what Allah wants." Muhid and his associates believe that Western societies are characterized by the values of selfish materialism and a quest for social status. They believe these values are corrupting young Muslims, and leading them astray from the desire to live for the sake of their religion. Should the youth become preoccupied with integration into secular UK society, these Islamists believe they will then lose their desire to know Allah and all that his religion commands—including the obligations to defend Islam through jihad and to work to install the supremacy of Allah's law. In short, these Islamists believe that the secular and liberal values that are actively promoted by the government are designed to defeat the very Islamic awakening they are trying to provoke.

The Masjid Dirar

AN IMPORTANT WEAPON, ACCORDING TO ISLAMISTS, IN THE GOVERNMENT'S "IDEOLOGI-cal war" on Muslims in the West is the promotion of interfaith dialogue—or what the extremists refer to as "joining of the religions" (*al-ittihad ad-diyan*). In this view, interfaith programs in local communities are encouraging young Muslims to embrace the principle that, as Abrahamic faiths, Islam, Judaism, and Christianity are equal—and to reject the idea that Islam is the superior ideology and way of life. The result, extremists fear, is that Muslim youth will fail to understand the imperatives upon them to work toward establishing Islam as the dominant power in society.

This issue was addressed in a lecture in May 2011 by the extremist activist Omar Brooks, a.k.a. Abu Izzudeen. A convert to Islam, Brooks was formerly known as Trevor Brooks. He was formerly affiliated with extremist Islamist groups "Al-Ghuraba" (The Strangers) and "al-Firqat un-Najiyah" (The Saved Sect), both of which have now disbanded. In 2008, Abu Izzudeen was sentenced to four-and-a-half years in prison for terrorist fundraising and inciting terrorism overseas, though he was released early on parole.

In a lecture entitled "The Misconceptions," which appeared on extremist web sites in May 2011, Abu Izzudeen criticized mosques in London that promote interfaith dialogue, and accused them of "selling out" by cooperating with authorities against the true interests of the Muslim community. In what appeared to be a specific reference to one mosque in East London, he said,

> This morning we were in the local *masjid*, in the gym underneath the masjid. And we heard the Imam give the call to *salat* [prayer]. And so sad for us—because that *masjid*, Masjid Dirar, is the *masjid* of what? Of inter-faith, and police, and spying on the Muslim community!"

> These [leaders of the mosque] are the ones who call for *al-ittihad ad-diyan*, the joining of the religions, between Jews and Muslims and Hindus and Christians. Shame on their face!...This will occur on the 27 May, when one of the top Rabbis will come down to discuss to the Muslims how we can join and unite with the *Juhud* [Jews]

One noteworthy aspect of this speech is Abu Izzudeen's reference to the story of Masjid Dirar, a mosque built in Medina during the life of the Prophet Mohammed. According to some accounts, the mosque was burnt down by the Prophet in 630AD after he learned that it was built by insincere Muslims who, unwilling to pray at a nearby mosque, sought to sow unbelief and dissent among the Muslim community by building their own mosque nearby. By invoking this story, it appears that Abu Izzudeen is attempting to show that there is historical precedent established by the Prophet himself that warrants violence against "insincere" Muslims who "sell out" to Western societies by participating in interfaith dialogue and other initiatives meant to divide the Muslim community.

Countering Prevent

THE ISLAMISTS APPEAR DETERMINED TO UNDERMINE THE IMPLEMENTATION OF THE UK government's Prevent strategy with a combination of strategic communication online and grassroots agitation among Muslim populations. In late May 2011, several days before the government published its revised Prevent strategy, Choudhary produced a booklet entitled *Islamic Prevent*.[5] This full-color, twenty-nine page document was distributed via Choudhary's website and designed to portray the government's counter-radicalization strategy as an attempt to replace Muslims' Islamic identity "with ideas which are not based upon the teachings of Islam." The document stated that it was "intended to open the eyes of Muslims and non-Muslims to the responsibility of Muslims living in the UK and to warn them of the dangers to their *Deen* [religion] from this UK Government-led campaign."

The report presents an eighteen-point plan to defend UK Muslim populations against what it calls "secular fundamentalism." It advocates that all Muslims should withdraw from engagement with non-Muslim society, and reject the British political and legal systems (voting in democratic elections and joining the police service are expressly prohibited.) The document further called on Muslims to remove CCTV camera networks from around mosques, which it claimed were part of Prevent-funded attempts to "spy on Muslims on behalf of the police and local authorities." It also calls for the creation throughout the UK of "mini-Emirates"—or self-policing, Muslim-majority enclaves where Sharia-based justice would be enforced.

Elsewhere, extremists have used the Internet to raise awareness of the perceived dangers of Prevent, and to dissuade UK Muslim youth from engaging with Prevent-funded community projects. The programs these extremists have singled out for criticism and rejection on Islamic grounds include youth outreach schemes, management training for mosque committees and Imams, British citizenship classes in local schools, and interfaith dialogue initiatives designed to encourage stronger community links between different faith groups.

Islamist ideologues and activists have moreover delivered Paltalk lectures and conducted online question-and-answer sessions with supporters to discuss Prevent and how Muslims should react to the implementation of government-funded programs in their communities. Guidance has been provided for young Muslims on how to identify the supposedly tell-tale signs of Prevent community engagement projects. One activist, Anthony Small (aka Abdul-Haqq Small), provided advice on his YouTube channel *Anthony Small Destroys Britain* for Muslims concerned that their local mosque may have "sold out" its community by accepting government sponsorship. Small, a former professional boxer and revert to Islam, called on Muslim youth to question their mosque's management committee about its outside sources of funding and support. If, Small claimed, the mosque had undertaken Home Office-funded mosque management training, then this would be evidence that the mosque had in effect become a local beach-head for the Prevent strategy.

In some Muslim communities, extremist groups such as Muslims Against Crusades have held marches and gatherings they call "Islamic Emirates roadshows." These are public proselytizing (*dawa*) events that are designed to raise an audience's general awareness of the imperative to implement Sharia and to promote Islamic self-governance in Muslim-majority areas. These roadshows have been accompanied by leaflet and sticker campaigns declaring certain neighborhoods as "Sharia-controlled zones" in which drugs, alcohol, music, and prostitution are forbidden. (There is generally little tolerance for open agitation by these types of extremists at many of the local mosques in the UK. Instead, these extremists operate on the fringes of the mosque in Islamic community centers, bookshops, sports facilities, and other places where young Muslims congregate.)

While much of this activism has been focused on London and the southeast of England, these Islamists are now also attempting to increase the scale of their *dawa* activities in other major UK towns and cities, including Liverpool, Birmingham, Cardiff, and Leicester.

Implications for the Extremists

THE RELATIVE STRENGTH OF THE ISLAMIST REACTION TO THE GOVERNMENT'S RE-LAUNCH of Prevent reflects the concern that it is more than simply a counterterrorism or counter-radicalization strategy. Rather, they argue that the government's new policies represent an existential-ideological challenge to British Muslims' fundamental understanding of Islam, as well to their own *raison-d'etre*—namely, the promotion of an Islamic awakening among the Muslim youth of the UK and Europe.

This raises a number of important questions, not only for Western governments and the national security community, but also for the extremists themselves. Given the severity of the threat that Islamists claim the Prevent strategy and the spread of "secular fundamentalism" poses to the "Islamic community," is the current Islamist response adequate? Or is the threat of "infidel society" to Islam now so existentially serious that it justifies a reaction that goes well beyond the normal Islamist response of missionary struggle (*dawa*) and non-violent activism? Viewed through the lens of Islamist ideology and the extremist understandings of Islamic jurisprudence, to what extent can a non-Muslim host government interfere with and constrict the propagation of Islam by its Muslim minority without obligating Muslims to employ new defensive measures—including violence?

Islamists regularly express frustration with what they perceive as the British government's double standards in their approach to policing Islamist activism. They often claim the government promotes freedom of speech and a right to protest, and yet labels as "extremist" anyone who exercises those rights by promoting Islamic issues or supporting their co-religionists defending Islam and Muslims around the world. They often claim that Muslims are being unfairly targeted by the government, and describe what they see as the government's attempts to and muzzle their missionary work.

This view was articulated by a British Islamist activist named Mizanur Rahman in an undated audio lecture entitled "Covenant of Security" that appeared on the Internet (references to security events occurring in the UK suggest it was recorded sometime 2006-2009):[6]

> Most of the people who are in prison are there not because they were trying to do something [i.e. terrorism] but because they read the wrong books. Or maybe they were camping in the Lake District—a bunch of homosexuals go camping and people say they're just having fun. Muslims go there, and they [authorities] are saying 'let's have a look on their computer—*Millat Ibrahim*,[7] very nice;' or they have another book about Jihad—'oh, what are they reading about Jihad for?'; or *The Forgotten Obligation*[8]—what are they reading these for? They must be in the Lake District training for Jihad.' They make these [books] illegal or censored to make sure they never come out...

> You aren't allowed to hear the opposite argument. That's their [the government's] idea of debate. They argue and 'say come and refute us—

but it's illegal to refute us. It's terrorism if you refute us. You go to prison. We will call the Mujahideen terrorists, murderers, barbaric. But if you say they're not, you're glorifying them.

Such frustrations have led Islamist activists to ask what their movement's response should be to what they perceive as government harassment and obstruction of their *dawa*.

In recent months, two closely connected themes have been especially prominent within extremist discussions. The first theme concerns the Islamic concept of the Covenant of Security (*Aqd Aman*), or the mutual non-aggression pact that many Islamists today believe exists between Muslims in the West and their non-Muslim hosts. Specifically, Islamists have begun to question whether the "ideological war" which, they allege, the UK government is waging against British Muslims, represents a breach of this covenant. The second theme concerns whether the UK should now be considered *dar al-harb*, an "abode of war" wherein Muslims and non-Muslims are in conflict.

In light of repeated terrorist attacks in the West by Al-Qaeda and its affiliates over the last decade, it might reasonably be assumed that the jihadist movement agreed to abrogate the covenant years ago. However, the issue in fact remains a source of significant disagreement among the broader jihadist movement's most respected shaykhs and scholars.[9]

The covenant most applicable to Muslims in the West is known as *Aman ul-Muslim*, which is a category of security covenant that applies to Muslims living as a minority among a non-Muslim majority or under a non-Muslim government. Such a covenant has a precedent in Islam's earliest years. In 615 AD, the Prophet Mohammed himself ruled that some of his Companions (*Sahabah*) who were suffering persecution by the pagan Quraish should seek temporary refuge within the domains of King Negus of Abyssinia, a Christian.

In their lectures and discussions, Islamist ideologues and *daees* (those engaged in *dawa*) in the UK routinely acknowledge the complexities and other sensitivities involved in any discussion of security covenants. Indeed, they often take care to set their inflammatory pronouncements on current affairs within the larger context of Islamic jurisprudence, which stresses the importance ascribed by Allah in the Quran to all covenants and acts of trust as well as the consequences in the afterlife for Muslims who betray them.[10] UK Islamists also consistently state their conviction that the Covenant of Security remains intact and that in general it is impermissible for Muslims living in the UK to breach that agreement. In principle, these Islamist rulings forbid all acts of terrorism on British soil by Muslims living in the UK.

Despite these assurances, a closer examination of UK Islamist discourse on covenants reveals a potentially more ambiguous position that may leave room for activists to reach their own conclusions about whether a covenant remains in place or not. The fact of such loopholes in Islamist jurisprudence may be of unique concern when viewed against the backdrop of the growing and concerted extremist opposition to the Prevent strategy, which, depending on its eventual impact, may be judged by some extremists as too much of an intrusion into their religious life and obligations to conduct *dawa*.

In study circles (*halaqas*) and lectures posted online or broadcast live via Paltalk, extremist preachers have reiterated their belief that a covenant between Muslims and British society remains in place in the UK. However, they also add that they respect the right of other Muslims to disagree with their position, and that no particular group's view on these matters is necessarily incorrect. Moreover, they refuse to reject the arguments of jihadist ideologues or leaders such as Anwar al-Awlaki and Ayman al-Zawahiri, who claim a Covenant of Security with the West no longer exists. Indeed, in such discussions, these preachers are often at pains to insist that their own views on Covenants of Security should not be interpreted as slandering or criticizing "the Mujahideen"—though they typically leave their audience to guess which groups or individuals they are referring to.

Anjem Choudhary offered an interesting perspective on Covenants of Security during a lecture entitled "Prevent Strategy" that appeared on the Internet in May 2011. At the end of a lengthy discussion on the government's counter-violent extremism policies, Choudhary was asked or his opinion on the Covenant. Like many other extremists, Choudhary responded by stressing that covenants had many conditions and were not to be made or broken with abandon. He spoke as well in broad terms about the importance of honoring a covenant, and the consequences for a Muslim in the afterlife of betraying such an agreement. He then explained the different types of covenants that applied to Muslims entering or living the UK:

> If you have an agreement with someone you have to honor it. Indeed it is a sign of *nifaq* [hypocrisy] to make an agreement with someone and then to break it. If someone comes into the country and the *kafir* says we will protect your life, wealth, etc. it is not allowed to kill them and take their wealth because that is an explicit covenant of security.[11]

> The implicit one is where if you apply for a driving license, a TV license, income support, housing benefit, the reason you apply for these is because you want some sort of protection. That's an implicit covenant of security.

Choudhary acknowledged that the issue of security covenants was complex and open to a range of interpretations, and he furthermore stressed that his own perspective should not be construed as a criticism of those Muslims who believed their co-religionists had no covenant of security with the West. He thus adopted the same ambiguous stance as many other fellow extremist preachers, stating that he both believes in the Covenant of Security in the UK while respecting the right of other Muslims to disagree and reject these terms:

> Imagine you didn't believe that there is no sanctity for the kuffar and his own life and wealth—someone like Anwar al-Awlaki and Shaykh Ayman al-Zawahiri who believe that there is no covenant anywhere in the West. That's why they say 'go to your mother's kitchen and make a cake.'[12] Not to eat, but to deliver to someone. [But] for us we say that's not allowed but we understand they have their opinion.

To underscore his position, Choudhary then invited his audience to consider the practicalities of living in the UK if they considered a Covenant of Security to be void:

> If you believe that the *kuffar* has no sanctity for his life and wealth and that this is a battlefield—dar al-harb—what is the *hukm* [ruling] to live among them and how should you live your life?

> He [Hadhrat Abu Basir] didn't live among the *kuffar*...he would raid and that's how he would make his living...he would live separately from them. You don't live next door to someone, brother, and in the morning say 'good morning Mr. Smith'; 'good morning brother Mohammed'; 'good evening Mr. Smith'; then the next morning it's 'goodbye Mr. Smith', and you kill him and take his wife [as your property]. This is called betrayal.

Choudhary's reference in his speech to the precedent of Hadhrat Abu Basir, a Companion of the Prophet Mohammed, is noteworthy. Abu Basir, who had been deeply angered by the early Muslims' agreement to the Treaty of Hudaybiyah in 628CE, relocated from Medina to the desert where he was not bound by any Covenant of Security and could therefore raid the supply trains of the pagan Quraysh with impunity.

Decoding the Extremists' Position

THE POSITION TAKEN BY CHOUDHARY ON THE COVENANT OF SECURITY IN THE UK has now been articulated by at least five other leading extremist *daees* and activists in recent months. But to what extent is this genuinely a reflection of their outlook? One interpretation of their rhetoric is that it has a basis in Islamic jurisprudence and may indeed reflect what these extremist leaders say to their supporters in private. Another interpretation is that their public stance is both expedient and intentionally deceptive. By stating support for the covenant they seek to avoid further interference by the authorities, while leaving a degree of ambiguity that could be interpreted by some of their followers as tacit endorsement for acts of domestic terrorism. Needless to say, neither of these interpretations is reassuring from the perspective of UK security.

The extremists' ambiguity on the covenant is clearly reflected in their rhetoric. In previous years, Islamist preachers such as Choudhary have refused to condemn the September 11, 2001 attacks in the U.S. and the July 7, 2005 attacks on the London transport system. Speaking to the BBC in August 2005, Abu Izzudeen called the 7/7 bombings "completely praiseworthy," though he claimed he was not personally calling for terrorist attacks on British soil. [13] Another long-standing activist, known as Abu Mounisa, delivered a speech at an Islamic conference in the UK in 2004 in which he appeared to glorify the 9/11 attacks, saying,

> When they talk about 9/11, when those two planes magnificently went through those buildings, and then people turn around and 'say hang on, that is barbaric'!

Clearly, the extremists' stance on the issue of the covenant remains opaque, and perhaps intentionally so. They state their support for a security covenant presumably to avoid further government interference in religious affairs, but they will nevertheless applaud—or at least not condemn—terrorist attacks on British soil when these do occur. By stressing that their opinion of the covenant is merely one of many Islamic opinions and that those disagreeing have made a potentially valid judgment, they allow their young supporters to draw their own, potentially dangerous conclusions from Islamic law. Their popular speeches, meanwhile, glorify terrorism.

Moreover, in his May 2011 lecture "Prevent Strategy," Choudhary explicitly stated that the extremists' stance on the covenant could change at any moment depending on the UK Government's domestic policy and the degree to which it constricts the Islamist movement's assorted efforts to spread its religious and political message:

> I believe in a Covenant of Security. But that could change. Shaykh Omar Abdelrahman of Egypt...he was in charge of *tanzim-ul-Jihad*...he said we used to carry *Dawa* in Egypt but when they fought us we declared *Jihad feesabilillah*. In other words, brother, we continue to carry *dawa*, [and] if they fight against us, if they become a group fighting against us here,

they don't allow us to carry *Dawa*, to carry Islam at all, it will be different brothers. We will fight back in that scenario. But if they leave us and allow us to practice and propagate Islam, we will continue [*dawa* and activism].

This raises a crucial question: To what extent will the further implementation of Prevent and the perception of increased government interference in the extremists' *dawa* be tolerated by the extremists before it forces them to abandon the covenant and non-violent activism altogether and embrace violent jihad?

It is difficult to determine where Choudhary and his associates may stand on this issue from their pronouncements alone. In one of his May 2011 lectures on UK counter-extremism, Choudhary explained to his audience that Muslims living under a non-Muslim government were obligated to practice their religion fully and without compromise. This included engaging in *dawa* to call people to Islam, and publicly condemning evil and corruption (*munkar*) in society:

> The purpose of having these covenants is so they can hear the word of Allah—if you are living among the *kuffar* then you carry *dawa* to them …you command good and forbid evil.

In effect, Choudhary argued that Muslims are permitted to enter into a security covenant with a majority non-Muslim government for the purposes of conducting *dawa*. Should the host government interfere with Muslims carrying out their fundamental religious obligations, then depending on the nature and severity of the infraction the potential implication from an Islamic viewpoint is that the government is violating the covenant. The further implication is that such interference, if it were deemed severe enough because it constricted the *dawa*, could justify in Islamic terms the abrogation of the Covenant of Security entirely.

Importantly, Islamist rhetoric today already portrays the UK government as clamping down on public dawa activities. This has especially been the case in recent years following the introduction of new anti-terrorism legislation that restricts public speech judged to incite or offer support for terrorism. Extremist political demonstrations display their aggressive interpretation of the Islamic principle of *al-wala wal-bara*, loyalty toward Muslims and enmity toward non-Muslims,[14] and this often places them at odds with British law on public order, "hate speech," and glorification of terrorism. This in turn provokes claims from the extremists that they have been unfairly victimized by the government merely for exercising a right to propagate Islam and challenge government policy through non-violent means.

Interestingly, Choudhary's comments on the conditions under which security covenants may be broken echo similar remarks made in 2005 by Shaykh Omar Bakri Mohammed, the former spiritual leader of Al-Muhajiroun who is still regarded as an Emir by many extremists in the UK. According to reports in the *Times* newspaper in July 2005, Bakri claimed in lectures delivered to students over the Internet that there was no longer a Covenant of Security in the UK and that Britain should be considered *dar al-harb*.[15] According to a *Times* report, Bakri did not specifically call for violent jihad in the UK, though he claimed that jihad was an obligation on all Muslims regardless of whether they lived in a Muslim country or not.

When challenged on his remarks by the *Times*, Bakri emphasized that he was speaking in "theoretical" terms. When asked by the *Times* to elaborate, he reportedly said:

> It means that Muslims can no longer be considered to have sanctity and security here [in the UK], therefore they should consider leaving this country and going back to their homelands. Otherwise they are under siege and obviously we do not want to see that we are living under siege.

As previously stated, one obvious interpretation of these statements is that Bakri and his associates are tacitly, if not explicitly, endorsing violence in the UK by declaring that Great Britain is *dar al-harb*. However, even under these conditions, an examination of the pronouncements of other extremists suggests that violent jihad is not necessarily an obligation.

In a lengthy lecture series offering an Islamic perspective on the subject of modern warfare, Mizanur Rahman addressed the subject of how countries are determined to be *dar al-harb* or *dar al-Islam* (an abode of Islam). He claimed that because there is no legitimate Islamic state anywhere in the world ruling solely through the complete application of Sharia, then the entire world is *de-facto dar al-harb* anyway:

> There is always going to be fighting...The Prophet Mohammed (s.a.w.) said 'I have been ordered to fight people until they testify *la illaha il-allah* ['there is no God but Allah'].

> There is always going to be two camps and two types of land and states and nations. Some nations will be dar al-harb—the land of war, where the Muslims will fight them until they say *La illahah ilallah* or until they agree to pay the *jizyah*. And there will be *dar al-Islam*. There are only two types—there is no third type. Some people get confused. They say 'how do you live in *dar al-harb*'—as if Saudi Arabia is *dar-al-Islam*!?

Saudi Arabia is *dar al-harb* as well. The whole world is *dar al-harb*. Because everwhere that Islam is not over the people is called *dar al-harb*. *Dar al-kufr* [disbelief], *dar al-shirk* [idolatry], *dar al-ridda* [apostasy]. These are all names of *dar al-harb*. The land of disbelief. The nation that's ruled by man-made law. In these nations there will always be fighting unless there's some kind of covenant or treaty to prevent them fighting.[16]

Crucially, however, Rahman then appeared to try to convince his audience that living in *dar al-harb* did not necessarily demand that a Muslim wage jihad through armed conflict. He went to considerable lengths to explain that other forms of jihad, such as the so-called "jihad of the tongue," represent critical contributions to the overall Islamic war effort. Within an Islamic context, Rahman introduced his students to important aspects of modern conflict such as psychological warfare:

War is more comprehensive than the glamorous....the thing we all dream about. To be that one in the foreign lands...Like Abu Dujanah[17] ...like Khalid bin Walid[18]...everyone wishes and dreams about this kind of reality. They want to be the next Khattab,[19] the next Abdel-Aziz al-Muqrin[20]—Abu Hajr. They want to be the next Saleh al-Awfi.[21] They don't understand everything that's involved. There is a need to understand the different types of war that are taking place. Sometimes the war is fought outside of the battlefield. And sometimes that is more fierce than the war itself.

In an effort to further clarify his position, he then suggested that "jihad of the tongue" should be the primary means of warfare for extremists in the UK:

How many times have our web sites been closed down? Even though we are not Mujahideen. We speak out—our Jihad is the Jihad of the tongue. Our role on the battlefield is that of the tongue. It's the debating, to challenge their [non-Muslims'] whole way of life. To challenge secularism. To challenge freedom. Still they won't even allow this to go on. That's their idea of debate.

This argument made by Rahman is, in fact, frequently deployed by extremists in the UK when discussing the relative benefits of activism and fighting. Naturally, this could be seen as a position of expediency and deception. However, the "jihad of the tongue" is widely seen by Salafist scholars and jurists as having a sound basis in Sharia and as a valid contribution to the overall Islamic jihad effort.

Conclusions

PRESENTLY, AL-MUHAJIROUN AND ITS SUCCESSORS SHOULD NOT BE VIEWED AS VIOLENT jihadist groups *per se*. Although many are proscribed in the UK, they are activist organizations, or more specifically *advocacy groups* focused on promoting an ideology close to that of the Al-Qaeda movement and mobilizing Muslim youth in support of the contemporary global jihadist agenda. The re-launch of the Prevent strategy by the UK Government is therefore seen by the extremists as a serious challenge to what they consider to be their duty as catalysts of a militant Islamist awakening. This concern is reflected in the strength of their response to Prevent both online and on the street. But how far will they go? What measures do they regard as permissible in order to defend against the feared secularization of their co-religionists? If today they genuinely consider their jihad to be a "jihad of the tongue," under what circumstances might this change?

The public statements of Islamist activists and leaders offer some clues to how to think about these questions, but no definitive answers. Currently their strongest consistent message is that a Covenant of Security exists in the UK, that terrorist attacks on British soil by those Muslims living there are in most circumstances impermissible, and that their most important contribution to jihad is one of rhetorical support and awareness-raising. This may well represent the view of most extremists at present—at least if one regards their public rhetoric as a fair reflection of their genuine juristic and ideological position.

An alternative analysis understands the extremists' public pronouncements as expedient and intentionally deceptive. In what is currently a restrictive legal and security environment, the extremists must continue to propagate their message in the UK while remaining under the threshold of prosecution under terrorism and hate crimes legislation. Therefore it is unlikely that these Islamists would ever call explicitly for violence in response to government efforts to clamp-down on their activities, even if they wanted to.

In any case, while these Islamists insist that they believe in a Covenant of Security in the UK, their jurisprudence and rhetoric reflect a much more ambiguous position on the matter. Activists like Anjem Choudhary and Mizanur Rahman have concluded that there are multiple legitimate Islamic understandings of security covenants, and they have simultaneously failed to refute the views of ideologues such as Anwar al-Awlaki and Al-Qaeda leaders. In effect, this provides a loophole for potential jihadists to draw their own understanding about covenants—and, by extension, their own conclusions about whether violence is permissible in the West today. Therefore, this ambiguous juristic and rhetorical position may be seen as a *de-facto* endorsement of the jihadist position on the validity of terrorist attacks in the West. Moreover, Choudhary has said that while he accepts the sanctity of the current Covenant of Security in the UK, this position could always change and the covenant could be abrogated if it is judged that British Government pressure has become so excessive that it constricts the ability of Islamists to conduct *dawa* and "jihad of the tongue."

The ambiguity of these Islamist figureheads already has been leveraged by their followers to add religious justification for acts of domestic terrorism. Movements such as Al-Muhajiroun have a proven track record of radicalizing young men to the point that they are willing to engage in jihadist violence both at home and abroad. According to Home Office figures, around fifteen percent of individuals convicted of offenses under the Terrorism Act between 1999 and 2009 had connections to Al-Muhajiroun. As one UK law enforcement official has said: "They [Al-Muhajiroun] might not be orchestrating terrorism, but they wind these young men up and then off they go on their own. Some of them end up doing stupid things."[22]

At the present time, it appears that many Islamist extremists in the UK are unwilling to carry out a terrorist attack on home soil, citing a Covenant of Security. For these extremists, the "jihad of the tongue" is and may well remain their primary focus. But given the ambiguous stance of extremist leaders on the covenant and matters of jihad, they have provided loopholes for their followers to draw their own conclusions about whether violent jihad is permissible for Muslims living in the West. These followers, in turn, may choose to act upon what jihadist ideologues such as Anwar al-Awlaki have claimed is the Islamic obligation to fight on all fronts.

What must also be acknowledged is the potential for the current positions and outlook of Islamist ideologues to change (and possibly rapidly) in reaction to new governmental and other external pressures. The UK Government's Prevent strategy has already been described by Islamists as an "ideological raid" and as part of a broader offensive against Islam. Insofar as these government efforts are understood by Islamists as constricting their *dawa* and jeopardizing their efforts to radicalize British youth, Islamist ideologues and their followers may be compelled to re-examine and possibly even abandon their present positions on the Covenant of Security as well as the impermissibility of violent jihad in the UK.

NOTES

1. Al-Muhajiroun is an Islamist extremist group in the UK founded by the Syrian ideologue Sheikh Omar Bakri Mohammed. The group has been officially disbanded, having been proscribed under UK terrorism legislation, but it continues to operate under a range of identities. The UK Government

has already proscribed several of these, including Islam4UK and the London School of Shariah.

2. The lecture formed part of a series that appeared on an extremist web site in 2010 addressing the fundamentals of Tawhid, including challenges to its implementation in a contemporary setting.

3. This statement was preceded by reference to several evidences including Surah 2 of the Quran (al-Baqarah), verse 219: "They ask thee concerning fighting in the Prohibited Month. Say: 'Fighting therein is a grave (offence); but graver is it in the sight of God to prevent access to the path of God, to deny Him, to prevent access to the Sacred Mosque, and drive out its members.' Tumult and oppression are worse than slaughter. Nor will they cease fighting you until they turn you back from your faith if they can [emphasis added]. And if any of you turn back from their faith and die in unbelief, their works will bear no fruit in this life and in the Hereafter; they will be companions of the Fire and will abide therein."

4. A reference to a 2004 report by the RAND Corporation that recommended supporting moderate Muslim groups as a bulwark against the propagation of radical Islamist ideologies, "Civil Democratic Islam: Partners, Resources, Strategies," RAND Corporation, 2004 http://www.rand.org/pubs/monograph_reports/MR1716/.

5. Copies of Islamic Prevent can be downloaded in PDF form from Choudhary's official web site: http://www.anjemchoudary.com/news/islamic-prevent.

6. Mizanur Rahman is a British national who was convicted in 2006 of inciting racial hatred, and in a 2007 retrial of solicitation to murder, after taking part in an Islamist extremist protest outside the Danish Embassy in London during which he is alleged to have called for the deaths of American soldiers in Afghanistan and Iraq. He completed four years of a six-year jail sentence. Following his release in 2010, he returned to Dawah activities and his lectures are widely promoted on the web site http://salafimedia.com.

7. *Millat Ibrahim* is a book by the influential Jordanian Jihadist ideologue Mohammed Taqir al-Barqawi, a.k.a. Abu Mohammed al-Maqdisi. An English-language copy can be found at http://www.e-prism.org/images/Millat_Ibrahim_-_English.pdf.

8. Possibly a reference to the book *The Absent Obligation (al-Farida al-Gha'iba)* by Mohammed Abdul-Saleem al-Faraj. A copy can be found at http://www.afghanvoice.com/Books/TheAbsentObligation.pdf.

9. For an examination of current perspectives on application of Covenants of Security in the West, see James Barclay, "Can Al-Qaeda Use Islam To Justify Jihad Against The United States? A debate In Progress," *Jamestown Foundation Terrorism Monitor*, Vol. 8, No. 25 (July 2010) http://www.jamestown.org/single/?no_cache=1&tx_ttnews%5Btt_news%5D=36562&tx_ttnews%5Bba ckPid%5D=381&cHash=1f9181c394 and "Jihadists Divided On Covenants Of Security," *Jane's Islamic Affairs Analyst*, May 2011.

10. Frequently-cited ayah and hadith underscoring the importance of covenants in Islam include:
"Oh you who believe! Fulfil your contracts." Al-Quran, Surah al-Maidah, verse 1.
"And purchase not a small gain at the cost of Allah's Covenant." Al-Quran, Surah an-Nahl, verse 95.
"There is no Eeman for the one who does not keep his covenant and no deen for the one who does not keep his trusts." (Ahmad).
"It is not allowed to take a small piece of wealth from the one you are in covenant with except if he is satisfied with that." (Abu Dawud).
"When Allah (swt) will gather the first and the last on the day of judgment, every betrayer will be raised with a banner. It will be said, This man is a betrayer...so and so, son of so and so."
(Sahih Muslim).

11. This is an *explicit* Covenant of Security, a specific type of covenant in which security in a non-Muslim country is sought and granted, for example through seeking asylum.

12. This is likely a reference to *Inspire*, an English-language magazine produced by Al-Qaeda in the Arabian Peninsula. Issue 1 of the magazine featured an article entitled *How to Make A Bomb In The Kitchen Of Your Mom*, http://publicintelligence.net/complete-inspire-al-qaeda-in-the-arabian-peninsula-aqap-magazine/.

13. For the BBC interview with Abu Izzudeen, see http://www.youtube.com/watch?v=uv704B93EZU&feature=player_embedded#!.

14. A particularly well-publicized example of this public agitation occurred in 2010 when members of an extremist group calling itself Muslims Against Crusades set fire to a pile of Remembrance poppies at an Armistice Day protest in Westminster, supposedly to draw attention to the killing of Muslim civilians by the British military in Afghanistan. At least one protestor was later convicted of offences under the Public Order Act. Extremists viewed these actions not as a publicity stunt, as some observers claimed, but as the practical application of Commanding Good and Forbidding Evil. See "Man Guilty Of Burning Poppies At Armistice Day Protest," *BBC News Online*, March 7, 2011. http://www.bbc.co.uk/news/uk-england-london-12664346.

15. For example, see *Omar Bakri Mohammed—A message Of Hate, The Times* newspaper, July 20, 2005.

16. Covenants of Security, Parts 1 and 2, by Abu Bara'a, can be found at: http://www.izharudeen.com/abu-bara-covenant-series.html.

17. Likely a reference to Abu Dujanah Simak bin Kharasha, a famous swordsman and Companion of the Prophet Mohammed who was killed in the Battle of Yamama in 632AD.

18. Famous Muslim general and Companion of the Prophet Mohammed, who led Muslim forces in successful military expeditions against the Roman and Persian Empires. Born in 592AD in Mecca, he died in 643AD in Homs, Syria.

19. Probably a reference to the Saudi guerrilla leader in Chechnya, Ibn al-Khattab, who led foreign fighters in the Caucasus until his death by poisoning in 2002.

20. Abdel-Aziz al-Muqrin (a.k.a. Abu Hajr) was a Saudi Jihadist who briefly led Al-Qaeda in the Arabian Peninsula during the group's most intensive period of activity in the Kingdom between 2003-2005. He assumed leadership of the group in 2003 but was killed in a shootout with Saudi security forces in 2004.

21. Saleh al-Awfi was a leader of Al-Qaeda in the Arabian Peninsula. He assumed command of the group in Saudi Arabia following the death in 2004 of Abdel-Aziz al-Muqrin. Al-Awfi was killed in a raid by Saudi security forces in Medina in 2005.

22. Author interview. Anonymity requested due to the sensitivity of the official's counterterrorism role.

Organization vs. Ideology: The Lessons from Southeast Asia

By David Martin Jones and M.L.R. Smith

THE NATURE AND EXTENT OF THE JIHADIST THREAT IN SOUTHEAST ASIA was not fully understood until well after the September 11, 2001 attacks on the United States. In the aftermath of those attacks, states in Southeast Asia appeared to move quickly to quash the putative threats in their own countries. Both the Singaporean and Malaysian authorities, for example, detained a number of suspected Islamist militants in late 2001.[1] Nevertheless, official and academic opinion remained for at least another year largely indifferent to the transnational terrorist network that had established itself in Southeast Asia.[2] This indifference and neglect was all the more surprising given the often intrusive intelligence agencies in many Southeast Asian countries. However, these too apparently failed to identify the evolving threat in their midst and the growing danger jihadism posed to regional order.[3] The October 2002 nightclub bombings in Bali, Indonesia, which killed 202 people, changed all of this. Those attacks brought to the world's attention the existence of a sophisticated, regionally-networked web of jihadist activity in Southeast Asia.

Prior to 9/11, regional intelligence cooperation was poor, and there was little awareness of or attention paid to the character and evolution of regional crime and terror networks. In particular, there existed a collective nescience concerning the growing ideological links between the most militant jihadist grouping in Southeast Asia, Jemaah Islamiah (JI), and the globalizing network of networks of Osama bin Laden's al-Qaeda.[4] One objective of this essay, therefore, is to indicate the process by which al-Qaeda and its regional affiliates attempted to draw localized separatist struggles in Southeast Asia into an evolving but loose network of transnational jihadism. To illustrate how this structure has advanced, we shall show how JI developed through kin groups, marital alliances, cliques, and radical *pesantren* (religious schools). Furthermore, we will examine the mix of counterterror strategies that have since 2003 successfully disrupted the organization and its network.

Exploring this evolving, networked organization in Southeast Asia also helps to illustrate a broader point about the character of modern jihadism. Long before it was appropriate to speak of an entity called al-Qaeda or the emergence of Osama bin Laden as its figurehead, those inspired by an Islamist, theo-political vision were already thinking strategically in terms of regional and transnational operations and their political effects. In Southeast Asia, we can trace this vision, if not also the strategy, back to the Darul Islam, or "Islamic Realm," movement. The vision born from Darul Islam's struggle against Dutch colonial rule was later influenced by Muslim Brotherhood ideologists like Said Qutb[5] and the Pakistani founder of Jaamat-i-Islami Abul ala Maududi. In time, the ideas of Abdullah Azzam (Osama bin Laden's ideological mentor, the so-called "Emir of Jihad") also shaped the evolution of Islamist thinking in Southeast Asia.[6] In fact, long before the end of the anti-Soviet jihadist struggle in Afghanistan, which is often cited as the first theater in which the contemporary Islamist *internationale* emerged,[7] pan-Islamist thinkers conceived resistance to modern *jahiliyya* (the state of ignorance) as a unified, global struggle that transcended local, state, and regional concerns. As Richard Engel has argued, the story of al-Qaeda is essentially about how "bin Laden tried to align with local militant groups with country-specific grievances to increase his global reach and influence."[8] In this context, JI provides an important case study of how a regional group came to share features of al-Qaeda's strategic thinking and developed links to it in the course of the 1990s—while at the same time retaining its own distinctive org-anization, character, and practice. Moreover, examining JI's origins, development, and disruption also provides an assessment of the relative importance of ideology, informality, and structure to sustaining organizations like JI that produce violence for strategic ends.

Examining JI, therefore, further allows us to test explanations that account for the behavior of contemporary violent jihadist organizations. In particular, we can analyze the extent to which the JI case supports the prevailing organizational approach to so-called terrorist behavior, which conceives terrorism as a definable and distinctive product rendered by groups or "firms." From this perspective, analysts often assume terrorist organizations either act instrumentally, using violence as a tacit form of bargaining to achieve political goals, or, alternatively, that they act "expressively," reflecting a need to "communicate" their politics in a particular and notably violent way.

In this regard, following Martha Crenshaw who considered terrorist violence "the product of the internal dynamics of the organization," Jessica Stern and Amit Modi contend that the primary goal of such organizations is survival.[9] The view of Stern and Modi, the endogenous, sociological perspective, rejects the "assumption that jihadist groups are most profitably categorized according to their ideology or mission." More precisely, "the group's ideology is just one of many variables a group can control in order to enhance its survivability. Indeed, one of the requirements for long-term survival is a flexible mission."[10] Audrey Kurth Cronin, who examines how so-called terrorism campaigns end—whether by decapitation, negotiation, strategic success, marginalization, repression, or reorientation—describes al-Qaeda as a remarkably agile organization with a fluid operational structure based on "a common mission statement and brilliant media campaign rather than standard operating procedures and a pervasive organizational structure."[11]

Yet, although al-Qaeda's tripartite structure of core, network, and periphery functions more like a social movement than a classic insurgent group, Cronin contends that "attraction to the mission or the ideology is a necessary but not a sufficient condition" in order to explain its network of associations.[12] From a related sociological perspective, Marc Sageman maintains that al-Qaeda and its affiliates like JI function as a "global salafi jihad," which is best viewed as "a social movement consisting of a set of more or less formal organizations linked in patterns of interaction."[13] Individual "hubs" form the basis of an informal, small world network that can resist "fragmentation because of its dense interconnectivity." Consequently, "a significant fraction of nodes can be randomly removed without much impact on its integrity."[14]

This network-centric approach to violent Islamist organizations, like the more conventional organizational approaches, also challenges the "theses of direct ideological appeals," emphasizing instead "the importance of social bonds during recruitment and conversion."[15] Max Abrahms perhaps summarizes this increasingly orthodox line of thought best, asserting that

> ...the preponderance of theoretical and empirical evidence is that people participate in terrorist organizations not to achieve their official political platforms, but to develop strong affective ties with fellow terrorists—an incentive structure reflected in the trade-offs terrorist organizations typically make to maintain their survival.[16]

By examining the JI's evolution as an organizational hub within the al-Qaeda network, we can thus evaluate whether Abrahms' somewhat adventurous claim is indeed true. In other words, is ideology or organization central to the survival of the group? Conversely, through the history of JI, we examine how such an organization might end, assessing what factors including decapitation, reorientation, and counter-radicalization contributed to its disruption. In order to do this we shall first trace the formation of JI, exploring the conditions that facilitated its organization and development up to 2002.

The Sources of the Organization

THE ROOTS OF JI AND THE REGIONAL NETWORK IT ESTABLISHED MAY BE TRACED to the 1970s and to two ethno-religious struggles in the Philippines and Indonesia. The guerrilla groups orchestrating these geographically separate struggles were eventually linked under the auspices of al-Qaeda in the early 1990s, when an increasingly interconnected global economy enabled the movement to emerge on an equally global scale.[17]

JI originated from a discontented faction within the proscribed Indonesian Islamist movement, *Darul Islam* (DI). After being exiled in Malaysia after 1985, the DI faction formed the organization al-Jamaah al-Islamiyyah, or the Islamic Society, in 1993 with the ultimate goal of establishing an Islamic state in President Suharto's New Order Indonesia.[18] Through links and exposure to the emerging Islamist *internationale,* thanks to Southeast Asian participation as Mujahedeen in the anti-Soviet Afghan struggle, the Indonesian JI leadership began to shift focus away from establishing an Islamic state in Indonesia to a wider, pan-Islamic agenda. This shift in strategic focus—which was primarily a consequence of changing ideology, rather than flexibility of mission— was the basis of a split that emerged between the founder of JI, Abdullah Sungkar, and the Indonesian-based DI leader, Ajengan Masduki. First, we will expose this broadening of the ideological and strategic mission through an exploration of the Indonesian and Malaysian complex that formed JI. Then, we will examine the movement's organizational links to the very differently organized groups that evolved in the 1970s in the Southern Philippines—groups with whom JI allied rather than integrated with during the course of the 1990s for the purpose of training, education, and strategic force multiplication.

The Indonesian Connection

IN THE 1990S THE INTERNATIONAL PRESS PORTRAYED SOUTHEAST ASIAN ISLAM AS politically moderate, genuinely friendly toward the West, and economically and developmentally focused.[19] This view seemed to capture the spirit of modern Malaysia under the dynamic "*Malaysia Boleh!*" (Malaysia Can Do It!) leadership of Mahathir Mohammad and modern Indonesia, a secular, nationalist state ruled along authoritarian, corporatist lines by Suharto's New Order (1966-1998). During the New Order era, Indonesia's majority Muslim population was represented mainly by two officially sanctioned organizations, the *Nahdlatul Ulama* (Islamic Scholars Awakening) and *Muhammadiyah* (Followers of Muhammad). With a combined membership of over seventy million, the leaders of these organizations promoted a politically quiescent, secularized, and tolerant Islamic doctrine of religious self-understanding.[20] Moreover, the concerns of these religious movements reflected national and practical concerns, even after Indonesia's democratic transformation. As the late Abdurrahman Wahid, the former *Nadhlatul* leader and Indonesia's first democratically elected president, observed in 2007, the New Order as well as its successor regime are preoccupied with "national development," and "give attention to only one thing, and that is [economic] growth."[21]

This more secularized understanding of religion notwithstanding, postcolonial Indonesia also incubated a more radical form of political Islam, which dated from the era of national resistance to Dutch colonial rule. Participation in the protracted twentieth-century struggles to liberate Indonesia from Dutch, Japanese, and once again Dutch rule after 1945 led to Maridjan Kartosuwijoro's Darul Islam (DI) movement to propose an Islamic constitution for the newly liberated Indonesian state. When the post-independence Indonesian government refused Islam a significant political or constitutional role, Kartosuwijoro formed the Tentera Islam Indonesia, or Islamic Indonesian Army, in West Java in 1948 to contest the secular nationalist Marhaenisme[22] promoted by Indonesia's first leader, President Sukarno. For the next thirteen years the DI's militias conducted a rebellion across the archipelago that culminated in Kartosuwijoro's arrest in 1962. The remnants of DI went on to enjoy a checkered relationship with the anti-communist New Order regime that ultimately replaced Sukarno in 1966. General Ali Moertopo, head of the New Order's special operations, briefly reconstituted DI after the fall of Saigon in 1975 to counter the potential revival of the Partai Kommunis Indonesia (PKI), or Communist Party of Indonesia.

Later, the government dismantled DI's paramilitary wing, *Komando Jihad* (Jihad Commandos), in 1977. Although some authors have linked Komando Jihad to a government attempt at destabilizing and discrediting moderate Muslim opposition to the New Order,[23] Komando Jihad still shared the uncompromising theology of, and geographical and family ties to, the founders of the DI movement. Among the 185 militants arrested in 1977 were Shaykh Abu Bakar Bashir and Abdullah Sungkar, who in 1971 had established the al-Mukmin *pesantren*, or religious school, near Solo, Central Java.[24] This *pesantren* would later form the basis for what Sidney Jones has termed the "Ngruki Network," which played the leading role in promulgating DI's and, subsequently, Jemaah Islamiyya's political vision of an Islamic state across the archipelago.[25]

From the outset, both Bashir and Sungkar rejected the secular, inclusive, and corporatist New Order ideology of *Pancasila* (Five Principles), and they railed incessantly against the regime.[26] Tried in 1982 and sentenced to nine years in prison for subversion, the pair escaped to the more religiously congenial Malaysia in 1985. With the financial assistance of sympathetic Malay businessmen, Bashir and Sungkar, together with an al-Mukmin graduate named Abu Jibril, established a school, hospital, and small Islamic community in the southern Malaysian state of Johor. The Lukmanul Hakiem school in Johor, like al-Mukmin in Solo, came to play a crucial role in both the ideological formation of and recruitment for the modern jihadist movement in Southeast Asia. Mukhlas, another al-Mukmin graduate and Afghan veteran, opened the Lukmanul school in 1991, and it soon became a center of gravity in the region for radicalism. Noordin Top—who would after the 2002 Bali bombings emerge as the leader of the Malaysian militant faction of JI—as well as his mentor, Dr. Azahari Husin, were in charge of organizing the Lukamanul school's curriculum before Malaysian authorities eventually closed the school in 2001.[27]

In 1993, the developing Malaysian network broke with their former DI mentors in Indonesia along specifically ideological lines. As Indonesia's former President Abdurrahman Wahid observed, JI was essentially a Malaysian creation. From this period, the Malaysian entity with Sungkar as its emir became formally known as "Al-Jamaah al-Islamiyyah." The JI organization formulated at this time a document describing the general guidelines of its struggle. Known as the Pedoman Umum Perjuangan al-Jamaah al-Islamiyyah (*PUPJI*, "General Guide for the Struggle of Al-Jamaah al-Islamiyyah"), the guidelines required all true Muslims and members of the group to strive to establish a *daulah Islamiah* (Islamic state) and identified the correct path or *dakwah* (Islamic missionary work) to achieve it. This required promoting education, enjoining good, forbidding evil, and ultimately, if necessary, armed jihad. Initially, the path mainly required resistance to the corrupt New Order regime in Indonesia. Later, this resistance call would come to include struggling against the "pharaohnic" rule of the governments in Singapore, Malaysia, and the Philippines. Abu Jibril, one of the lead architects of this expansive strategy, envisaged the eventual transformation of Southeast Asia into a "Daulah Islam Nusantara," or an Islamic archipelago.[28]

The PUPJI outlined an ambitious three-stage process of political transformation. The first stage required preparation to establish the *daulah,* or the Islamic state; the second required the organization of the *daulah*; and the final stage required the reformed Islamic state to lead the Muslim world into a politically integrated, caliphate-centered, and religiously-inspired epoch. The crucial first step in this transformative process required a vanguard (*Jemaah*, or group) with a righteous or correct leadership carefully grooming its membership. JI's initial leadership included Sungkar, Bashir, Faiz Bafana (who had migrated to the group from Jakarta), and Abu Jibril. Another Javanese cleric, Nurjaman Riduan Isamuddin, also known as Hambali, had joined them in the 1980s. Hambali was a disciple of Sungkar, and as a consequence of Sungkar's mentoring was selected to train with the Mujahedeen in Afghanistan and Pakistan between 1986 and 1987.[29]

In Peshawar through the good offices of Abdullah Azzam's MaK, the precursor of al-Qaeda, Hambali along with Bafana and approximately fifty graduates of the Jemaah project networked with an international movement of radicals inspired by the Mujahedeen's struggle against the Soviet occupation of Afghanistan. These fighters included Zulkarnaen, who subsequently led JI's military wing, as well as a desultory mixture of Southeast Asians from Indonesia, Malaysia, and the Philippines. Hambali returned to Malaysia briefly in 1987 before leaving for Mindanao in the Philippines where he developed links with the Moro Islamic Liberation Front (MILF) and their tactically important Abubakar training camp in Southern Mindanao.

In the course of the 1990s, JI evolved into an ideological hybrid that derived its theology and strategy in part from the Egyptian Islamic jihadi groups Gamaa al-Islamiyah al-Masri (Al-Masri Islamic Group) and al-Islamiyah al-Jihad al-Masri (Al-Masri Islamic Jihad),[30] as well as from its own DI-influenced indigenous resources. JI entertained Ayman al-Zawahiri in Malaysia in the mid-1990s, and Sungkar and Bashir both visited Pakistan. Al-Zawahiri was al-Qaeda's number two and the theorist of globalizing the Islamist struggle against *kuffar* (infidel) regimes. Sungkar also met bin Laden on three occasions between 1990 and 1997. Moreover, by 1999 Hambali had emerged as an increasingly significant figure on al-Qaeda's Military Command Council.[31]

These personal ties in this small multinational network developed as a consequence of shared and intensifying ideological understanding. Rather than demonstrating mission flexibility or a contingent relationship formed from close social bonds, the intensification and increasingly global ambitions of their shared ideology constituted for both groups the basis of their cooperation as well the cause of the breach between DI and JI.

It was also in the course of the 1990s that Sungkar, Abu Jibril, Hambali, Azahari Hussin, Noordin Top, and others formed the Kumpulan Mujahidin Malaysia (KMM, or Malaysian Mujahideed Movement) franchise along with elements from earlier Malay postcolonial era Islamist groups that had violent Gnostic tendencies.[32] The Malaysian arm of JI also actively pursued its regional strategy of forging alliances with groups that shared its ideology and jihadist *modus operandi*. In the Philippines, for example, it established links with the Moro Islamic Liberation Front and the recently-formed Moro National Liberation Front (MNLF) splinter group, Abu Sayyaf (Sword of God).

The PUPJI further outlined the structure of the organization. As emir, Abdullah Sungkar presided over and appointed a governing council (Markaz). In 1998 the Markaz consisted of Sungkar, Bashir, Mukhlas, Abu Rusdan (the son of a jailed DI activist), and Zulkarnaen. This council took responsibility for education, training, fund-raising and internationalization of their plans. The central command of the council oversaw four regional spheres of operation known as *mantiqi*.[33] Hambali was responsible for Mantiqi 1, which was comprised of Malaysia and Singapore. Fati, an Indonesian, headed Mantiqi

2, which extended across Western Indonesia. Nasir Abbas, Mukhlas' brother-in-law, assumed responsibility for Mantiqi 3, which included the Philippine province of Mindanao, Indonesian Sulawesi, and the West Malaysian state of Sabah. Meanwhile the al-Mukmin graduate, Abdul Rahim Ayub, who married an Australian Protestant convert to Islam, Rabiah Hutchinson, led Mantiqi 4, comprised of Papua and Australia.[34] The mantiqis were subdivided into *wakalah*s, or delegated agencies. Thus Mantiqi 1 consisted of four *wakalah*s—Perak, Johor, Kuala Lumpur and Singapore—and each of these possessed its own internal command structure.

According to Sidney Jones' International Crisis Group report, it is plausible to view this structure as essentially military with "brigades (*mantiqi*), battalions (*wakalah*), companies (*khatibah*), platoons (*quirdas*), and squads (*Fiah*)."[35] JI also possessed at least one special operations group (*Laskar Khos*), which would later be responsible for the 2003 Marriott Hotel bombing in Jakarta. Despite the hierarchical character of the organization, which rendered it ultimately more friable than the al-Qaeda movement, the Mantiqi structure nevertheless allowed for a considerable degree of regional latitude in both planning and operations.

After 1998, as JI's hierarchical organizational structure further took shape, links between JI and the ongoing jihad in the Philippines developed dramatically. Mantiqi 1 sent groups of Malaysians and Singaporeans to MILF training camps. Al-Mukmin graduate Fathur Rahman al-Ghozi became the primary JI contact for both MILF and Abu Sayyaf.[36] Al-Ghozi had made at least two training trips to Afghanistan to further his studies. At the same time, contacts between JI and al-Qaeda in Afghanistan also appreciably deepened. Hambali notably developed ties with Khalid Sheikh Mohammed, al-Qaeda's man in the Philippines, while several JI personnel regularly visited Kabul.

Consequently, JI was well-poised to act in 1997 when the Asian Financial Crisis struck. The crisis undermined the legitimacy of the New Order regime in Indonesia and damaged the authority of the United Malay National Organization (UMNO)-led multiethnic coalition that had governed the Malaysian federation since its inception in 1963. JI and its affiliates subsequently began to exploit regional political and economic uncertainty in the interests of jihad against both the secular enemy within and the far enemy in Washington.

In this context, JI Malaysia engineered a crucial connection between al-Qaeda and KMM that facilitated the 9/11 attack. At this juncture, Yazid Sufaat, a former Malaysian army officer who by the 1990s had significant business interests tied to companies in Kuala Lumpur (such as Green Laboratories and Infocus Technologies), became a significant benefactor of Malaysian Islamism.[37] In January 2000, Sufaat hosted the Pentagon hijackers Khalid Al-Midhar and Nawaq Alhamzi.[38] Later, in October 2000, he met with Zacarias Moussaoui in the same condominium. At this meeting he provided Moussaoui with funds and papers to enter the United States as an Infocus Technologies "marketing consultant." Moussaoui was later tried and convicted in the U.S. for his role in the September 11 attacks. Also in October 2000, Sufaat purchased four tons of ammonium nitrate for Fathur Rahman al-Ghozi to carry out a regional bombing campaign (in March 2003 Malaysian police found most of the explosives stashed in a plantation near Muar).[39]

Over the same period, the Malaysian connection extended its reach into Singapore via mosques across the causeway in Johor Baru. Mas Selamat Kastari oversaw the Singapore link while Ibrahim Maidin coordinated the JI cell in the city-state. Ibrahim Maidin had spent three weeks training in Afghanistan in 1993 and had in 1999 written to Osama bin Laden and Mullah Omar, the head of the Taliban in Afghanistan, seeking spiritual and ideological guidance.[40] From the early 1990s Maidin held religious classes in Singapore, which doubled as a recruitment center for the JI cells he established there.[41]

The collapse of Suharto's New Order regime in 1998 further facilitated the extension of regional and international connections and operations. By the end of 1998, Sungkar, Bashir, Hambali, and Abu Jibril left Malaysia and returned to Indonesia to organize and reinvigorate the jihad there. In other words, regional political disorder and economic uncertainty contributed an important variable, as we shall subsequently show, to the development of JI's operational outreach and its ideological appeal.

In 1999, however, Sungkar died and Bashir assumed the role of emir. Sungkar's loss, which was unremarked at the time and neglected in later accounts, significantly affected group cohesion, occasioning a developing factionalism in the JI leadership group that volatized the organization particularly after the Bali bombings of 2002. Those associated with the comparatively less militant Bashir faction increasingly identified and promulgated a non-violent political route to achieving an Islamic state. In August 2000 Bashir established the Majlis Mujahedeen Indonesia (MMI, Indonesia Mujahideen Council) in Jakarta to advance cooperation among ideologically like-minded Indonesian Islamist groups such as the Front Pembela Islam (Islamic Defenders Front) and the recently established regional branch of the international Islamist movement, Hizb-ut Tahrir (Party of Liberation).[42] By contrast, the more militant members of Hambali's Mantiqi 1 faction found Bashir's political links and his ties to the former Indonesian Deputy President Hamzah Haz antithetical to Sungkar's PUPJI and the secretive, underground, violent, vanguard strategy of resistance and jihad that the guidelines supported. It should, however, be emphasized that this evolving split affected tactics rather than the overall strategy or worldview of the radicals. Both Bashir and Hambali promulgated Islamist ideas, and despite Bashir's promotion of a more robust political agenda, he never disavowed the use of violence—although he might dissimulate it, subscribing to the casuistic principle that "deception in war is valid."[43]

Despite the evolving disagreement over tactics and personalities, the relative openness of Indonesian politics after 1998 and the collapse of internal security coordination, especially during the brief presidency of moderate Islamic leader Abdurrahman Wahid between 1999 and 2001, enabled JI in Indonesia to consolidate linkages with cells in Malaysia, the Philippines and Singapore. In 2000, JI created Rabitat ul-Mujahideen (Legion of Mujahideen), an umbrella of Islamist groups conducting armed struggle against secular regimes in the region. The putative network included MILF and Abu Sayyaf in the Philippines, Rohingya Solidarity Organization in Burma/Myanmar, Gerakan Aceh Merdeka (GAM, Free Aceh Movement), and Jemaah Salafayya (Salafist Group) in Thailand.

Significantly, while links with the Philippines and Malaysia flourished, GAM ultimately rejected JI's overtures. At the same time, the long-standing Pattani United Liberation Organization (PULO) separatists' resistance in Southern Thailand restricted JI's influence to a minimum and resisted incorporation into a regional jihadist enterprise. Similarly in Indonesia itself, Jafar Umar Thalib's Laskar Jihad (Army of Jihad), a Javanese group devoted to the Islamist struggle against Christians in Sulawesi, also rejected JI's advances. Although Jafar fell out spectacularly with what he considered Abu Jibril's self-aggrandizing behavior towards the Sulawesi jihad, their disagreement was primarily over strategy and not merely a clash of personality. This constituted the crucial variable explaining Laskar Jihad's rejection of JI's overtures. Analogously, the leadership of the insurgencies in both Southern Thailand and Aceh also saw little strategic value in networking with JI or al-Qaeda to advance their strategically limited goal of achieving liberation from the postcolonial arrangements that constrained their respective peoples. In the same way, Laskar Jihad sought to maintain and extend Islamism in Sulawesi, and Jafar thus rejected cooption into a regional, global campaign. In other words, strategy and ideology ultimately trumped social connections in the development of JI.

By contrast, in the Philippines and Malaysia a shared ideological vision adumbrated by close personal contacts advanced the integration of regional strategy into a wider, transnational Islamist agenda. In this context, the roles played by key al-Qaeda figures were providential. Khalid Sheikh Mohammed regularly visited the Philippines where Ramzi Youssef, the first World Trade Center bomber, was based. With him in the Philippines was Hambali, who coordinated JI's regional strategic thinking and who, as mentioned above, also held a significant position on the Military Command Council of al-Qaeda. The political uncertainty that gripped Indonesia after the 1997 financial crisis particularly facilitated these developments The Indonesian armed forces, the TNI, responsible under the New Order for the dual function (*dwifungsi*) of external security and for preserving national integrity, lost its privileged political role as well as its political autonomy after 1998. It also suffered from internal divisions. Meanwhile, the Kepolisan Negara Republik Indonesia (Indonesia National Police) (*POLRI*), which after 1998 assumed responsibility for national security, was unprepared and under-resourced for the task of maintaining internal security.

The JI and the MMI consequently exploited the uncertain transition in internal security arrangements to recruit fighters and sponsor inter-communal violence in Ambon, Maluku, and Sulawesi. Moreover, after the Philippine military overran Camp Abubakar in Mindanao, JI had, in this relatively short period, acquired the resources and capacity to establish its own training camps in Poso, Central Sulawesi by 2000. In December the same year, Hambali organized attacks on Christian churches across Java—the most widespread terror attacks in Indonesian history, which bore the al-Qaeda signature of multiple coordinated targeting.[44] Involved in Hambali's Indonesian terror campaign were al-Mukmin graduates Mukhlas, who also operated under the *nom de guerre* Ali Gufron, Imam Samudra and Mukhlas' brother, Amrozi bin Nurhasyim. The same team was also involved in bombing a church in Batam in January 2001. By 2001, Hambali had established himself as the effective chief executive officer for JI terror operations, coordinating a network within the wider JI and MMI franchises. This militant tendency within JI reached the apex of both its power and regional influence in early 2002.[45]

To sum up, the evolution of JI as a terror organization required close interpersonal ties, as well as historic links to an Islamist ideology of a local provenance. Nevertheless, it was the projection of that ideology onto a global canvas, together with the strategy necessary to achieve it, that drove JI first as a school and then as a regional movement with an increasing commitment to violence to define itself as a distinctive organization. Moreover, the political crisis engendered by the financial meltdown of the region after 1997 provided the contingent circumstances for the group to flourish, despite growing factionalism and interpersonal friction within the hierarchically ordered group.

The Philippine Connection

ALTHOUGH JI IS ESSENTIALLY A MALAYSIAN-INDONESIAN CREATION, AFTER 1998 IT developed a capacity to integrate operations across Indonesia, Malaysia, Singapore, Thailand, and the Philippines. The Philippine connection in Mindanao, with its long-standing Moro resistance movement against the Catholic Philippine state, was particularly important for both JI and al-Qaeda's regional force multiplication. The long established MILF training camp, Abubakar, played a vital role in the education and training of successive generations of Mujahideen, and al-Qaeda early recognized the importance of Moro separatism to transnational strategic thinking. Sustained Moro resistance dates from the 1950s, but it became increasingly internationally networked in the course of the 1970s with the emergence of the MILF and later with Abu Sayyaf, the violent splinter group that broke away from the MNLF in 1991. (The precise circumstances surrounding Abu Sayyaf's emergence remain somewhat obscure.)[46]

From the late 1980s, both MILF and, after 1991, Abu Sayyaf received direct support from al-Qaeda. In 1988 Mohammed Jamal Khalifa, Osama bin Laden's brother-in-law, established a number of businesses in Manila that supplied financial and logistical support to Abu Sayyaf and MILF.[47] Khalifa's front organizations included E.T. Dizon Travel—active in shipping goods between the Philippines, Malaysia, the Netherlands, and Saudi Arabia—as well as Dizon Realty. Khalifa also established non-governmental organizations and charities that laundered money for local resistance like the International Islamic Relief Organization (IIRO).[48] Through these organizations Khalifa established further links to Libya and the Groupe Islamique Armée (Islamic Army Group) in Algeria. Khalifa's philanthropy also enabled Abu Sayyaf personnel to study at Madaris in Pakistan. Khalifa left Manila in 1995.

The revenues from these enterprises also financed training centers like camp Abubakar in Mindanao in the Southern Philippines.[49] Until the Philippine army overran it in 2000, the camp provided instruction for explosives and assassination techniques. By the mid-1990s the camp regularly attracted Mujahideen expertise from Pakistan, Afghanistan, and Algeria to train local militants.[50] In 1998, al-Qaeda sent a Sudanese colonel, Ahmad al-Gamen, to Mindanao to train MILF members to use explosives and commando techniques.[51] The process was two-way. In 2002, the former leader of the counterterrorism task force of the Philippine National Police, Senior Superintendent Rodolfo Mendoza, observed that, "there were foreign nationals like French Algerians, Egyptians, and Pakistanis who were trained by Filipinos inside Camp Abubakar."[52] Camp Abubakar maintained its international profile and was internally sub-divided into Algerian, Palestinian, and other sections. From 1996 the Indonesian JI contingent trained within the sprawling complex of Camp Hudaibayah. Hudaibayah was in turn divided into "tribes" known as Camp Solo, Camp Banten, and Camp Sulawesi.

In 1998 and 1999, while the Abubakar complex still remained in operation, bin Laden facilitated links between the Algerian GIA and the MILF's leader, Salamat Hashim.[53] The Philippine Directorate of Intelligence maintained that "sometime last mid-February 1999 Osama bin Laden reportedly contacted separately MILF chairman Salamat and the Algerian leader Hassan Hattab. Bin Laden reportedly sought the assistance of Salamat in establishing new camps in Mindanao and instructed Hattab to start operations."[54]

Prior to this development as early as 1991, Khalifa had forged particularly close ties with Abdulrajak Janjalani, the founder of Abu Sayyaf. Janjalani, a former schoolteacher who had spent time in Saudi Arabia and Afghanistan where he met Osama bin Laden, formed Abu Sayyaf from former MNLF fighters in his native Basilan in the Southern Philippines. Bin Laden supported Janjalani's group with a donation of $US 6 million. From the outset, Abu Sayyaf shared al-Qaeda's and JI's vision of creating a pan-Islamic realm, the *Daulah Islamiyah Nusantara*.[55] Their ambitions deviated profoundly from the far more circumscribed separatist political goals of both the MILF and MNLF. Abu Sayyaf also shared al-Qaeda's jihadist approach to realizing a transnational Islamist utopia. In this context after 1991, Abu Sayyaf embarked upon an increasingly violent campaign of bombings, kidnappings, rapes, and extortion across the Southern Philippines. Janjalani's links to al-Qaeda's Philippine contacts along with Middle East-linked Khalid Sheikh Mohammed and Ramzi Yousef facilitated Abu Sayyaf's pursuit of polymorphous violence.

Like most elite Islamist international activists, Yousef—a Baluchi, Swansea University-educated science graduate based in the Philippines[56]—possessed multiple identities and traveled on a variety of passports, including an Iraqi one. Yousef planned the first World Trade Center bombing in 1993.[57] His putative uncle, also a Baluchi Sunni, Khalid Sheikh Mohammed, was by 2001 number three in the al-Qaeda hierarchy and featured in both the planning of 9/11 and later JI operations.[58] From 1992, both Yousef and Khalid Sheikh Mohammed took regular scuba diving trips to Puerta Galera in Basilan in order to train with the Abu Sayyaf and develop its tactical and strategic thinking. In December 1994, Abu Sayyaf claimed responsibility for Yousef's failed attempt to bomb Philippine Airlines Flight 434 from Cebu. The bombing was a test run for Yousef's grand plan, Operation Bojinka, to explode eleven passenger planes over the Pacific en route to Los Angeles. A fire at Yousef's apartment followed by a police raid and Yousef's arrest, however, disrupted the operation in January 1995.[59] Yousef had also planned to assassinate the Pope during his visit to the Philippines in 1995.[60] The subsequent arrest and interrogation of Abdul Karim Murad in Pakistan in March 1995 who operated under Ramzi Yousef's guidance confirmed the bin Laden connection.[61] Through Yousef and Khalid Sheikh Mohammed, Osama bin Laden's imprimatur was clearly visible in the Abu Sayyaf's political vision and strategic style. Indeed, the loose al-Qaeda franchise model served as the basic organizational principle for Abu Sayyaf.

Notwithstanding the disruption of Operation Bojinka, Abu Sayyaf subsequently conducted a beachhead assault on the town of Ipil in Mindanao in April 1995. However, links with al-Qaeda deteriorated after 1998 when the Philippine National Police killed Abdurajak Janjalani in a firefight on Basilan Island. Janjalani's younger brother, Khadaffy, assumed the leadership of the group, which increasingly resorted to kidnappings and hostage takings to subsidize its activities. In 2000 it expanded these operations to the West Malaysian dive resort of Sipadan where they took 21 hostages. Apart from a ransom, they demanded the release of Ramzi Yousef, detained in the U.S., in exchange for the hostages. The abduction of 20 hostages from an upscale resort on the "safe" Southern Philippine resort island of Palawan followed in May 2001. A year after the raid, a botched Philippine army rescue saw two of the hostages, including the American missionary, Martin Burnham, killed and the rest of the hostages wounded. The kidnappers subsequently escaped.

Khadaffy's pattern of random kidnapping, ransom demands, and polymorphous violence culminated in the bombing of the Manila Superferry on February 14, 2004 with the death of 116 passengers. Abu Sayyaf apparently bombed the ferry because the owners refused to pay protection money. Despite its continuing links to JI, Abu Sayyaf under Khadaffy's leadership became increasingly fragmented and assumed the identity of a violent criminal gang with Islamist characteristics. Abu Sayyaf's degeneration into banditry and raiding explains the divergent estimates of the size of the group, which range from 200 to over 2000 members.

Abu Sayyaf's variable membership, however, reflected the group's roots in the alliance system traditionally practiced amongst the Tausug and Yakun ethnic minorities that inhabited the Basilan and Jolo islands. In the case of both JI and Abu Sayyaf, kinship ties constituted an important component to the evolution and security of the group. In other words, JI, Abu Sayyaf, and al-Qaeda's small world network was ideological in its formation but came to depend increasingly upon social bonds and interpersonal ties. JI and to a lesser extent Abu Sayyaf possessed formal, hierarchical, and informal characteristics. JI functioned primarily as a school while Abu Sayyaf emerged from kinship ties. Indeed, kinship and marriage facilitated the deeper integration of the network.

Kinship, Marriage and Terror Networking

THE EVOLUTION OF JI AS A VIOLENT TRANSNATIONAL ISLAMIST GROUP UP UNTIL 2002 demonstrated its capacity to ideologically insinuate itself into seemingly self-contained conflicts. It developed what Jessica Stern has termed, "friendships of convenience."[62] It also demonstrated the extent to which local groupings were willing to receive al-Qaeda's largesse and support to sustain their resistance.

In organizational terms however, relations between JI, Abu Sayyaf, and al-Qaeda were largely protean, informal and personal. Although facilitated by the revolution in global communications, their connectivity increasingly depended on ethnic and kinship ties and marital alliances. In the case of Abu Sayyaf, both kin and clan ties played and continue to play a crucial role in the structure of the group and explain its pattern of violence. In his classic study of the Tausug minority in Jolo and Basilan (Southern Mindanao) in the 1960s, Thomas Kiefer observed how the local alliance system constituted the building block of political organization, particularly in relation to warfare. Dyadic friendship relations and ties of reciprocity "involving the exchange of political and military services, goods, and affect" enabled the formation of armed bands. Here minimal alliances founded on close kin ties like the Janjalani brothers and their in-laws formed the basic group, while medial alliances formed through the dyadic relationship between two minimal kin groups constituted mid-level alliances. Finally, a maximal alliance involving regional affiliations formed the apex of the Tausug warfare system. By the 1960s the developing power of the postcolonial state had effectively disrupted the formation of maximal alliances.[63]

However, for purposes of resistance and political organization, medial and minimal alliances remained intact. Facilitated by the technology and training that al-Qaeda made possible, Abu Sayyaf deployed this medial and minimal alliance system to conduct operations and afterwards melt back into the civilian population.[64] Its capacity to network with like-minded alliances in both Afghanistan and Indonesia further enhanced its regional and transnational cachet. The globalization of the 1990s that opened borders and accelerated communication quickened the process, particularly with respect to the evolving connections to the far more hierarchical and elitist JI.

Consequently, a number of factors in the course of the 1990s may be identified as critical to the organization and development of the JI and Abu Sayyaf networks. The first was the evolution of an ideology that considered jihad as a duty to bring about a radical millennial transformation of both the regional and international orders. The second was access to training camps and schools to recruit and indoctrinate a generation of true believers. Access to camps and funding from Saudi charities and Afghanistan helped develop training camps like Abubakar in the Philippines and schools like Lukmanul and Ngruki that formed the core of the JI structure. Yet, the training and funding was reinforced by close and evolving interpersonal and kin ties. Unlike the very specific Tausug ethnicity that formed the backbone of Abu Sayyaf, most of the JI leadership hailed from Indonesian, Hadrami backgrounds and often retained Yemeni kinship and religious connections. JI membership also demonstrated close ties to the DI movement of the 1950s. Thus, Fathur Rahman al-Ghozi's father was a DI member imprisoned by the New Order regime. The family of Ahmed Kandai exhibited a jihadist genealogy. Kandai belonged to DI and had attempted to assassinate Sukarno in 1957. His brother Natsir worked closely with both Sungkar and Bashir in Central Java and Malaysia. Kandai's three sons all became jihadists. Two of them took part in the bombing of the Philippine Ambassador's residence in Jakarta in January 2000, while the third bombed the Atrium shopping mall, Manila, in the same year. Interestingly, brothers are a notable feature of JI: apart from the Bali bombers, al-Ghozi, and his brother, Hambali's brother Rusman Gunawan acted as a conduit for emails between al-Qaeda and Hambali and he participated in the Jakarta Marriott Hotel bombing of 2003.

Inter-marriage further reinforced the JI membership and kept the network secure. Thus Mukhlas married head of Mantiqi 3 Nasir Abbas' sister, while al-Ghozi and Amrozi are in-laws. After the police shot al-Ghozi in 2003, his younger brother, also a member of JI, married his widow. Abdullah Sungkar married two of his step-daughters to Ferial Muchlis Abdul Halim, head of a Selangor JI cell, and Syawal Yassin, a prominent Sulawesi jihadi. Sungkar also celebrated the marriage between Abdul Rahyim Ayub and Australian Rabiah Hutchinson. Haris Fadillah, a DI militia leader in Ambon, married his daughter Augustina to Indonesia-based al-Qaeda representative Omar al-Faruq. Somewhat differently, Australian "Jihad" Jack Thomas married Indonesian Maryati on the advice of JI friends.[65]

Kith, kinship, and exogenous marriage ties therefore facilitated the network's proliferation and the promulgation of its ideology. Intermarriage extended JI's links from Afghanistan through Malaysia and Indonesia to Sydney and Melbourne. At the same time, this long-gestating Islamist *qabilah* (tribe) dedicated to transforming the region into a *daulah Islam* spread their message using modern communications systems: it was determined to transcend the nation-state in order to forge a transnational network that created a virtual Islamic realm with the potential to disrupt, disorganize, paralyze, and terrorize insecure postcolonial states. Globalization of communication facilitated these interconnections, while funding from a variety of sources including remittances, ransoms, charities, and front organizations lubricated the process. For instance, according to FBI section chief Dennis Lormel, clandestine funds found their way from the Middle East into Southeast Asia through the operation of Saudi-sponsored charity organizations. After 1999, the JI successfully embedded members or "coopted Saudi charities (al-Haramain and IIRO), their Indonesian counterparts (Komite Aksi Penanggulangan Akibat Krisis, or KOMPAK, Crisis Prevention Committee), and the Medical Emergency Relief Charity (MERC) that was used to support militant activities."[66] In August 2006, the U.S. Treasury belatedly identified the IIRO's Indonesian and Philippine offices as "facilitating fund raising for al-Qaeda and affiliated terrorist groups."[67]

Countdown to Bali

ONLY THE DISCOVERY OF JI'S VIDEO PLAN TO ATTACK WESTERN EMBASSIES IN DECEMBER 2001 exposed JI, the al-Mukmin, and Lukmanul schools' unorthodox curricula activities. Somewhat fortuitously, an American soldier stumbled upon the video in the rubble of al-Qaeda's headquarters in Kabul following the U.S.-led attack on Afghanistan.[68] It also emerged that the Changi naval base and several other installations in Singapore, including the main civilian airport, were also on JI's target list.[69] As a result of this accidental discovery, al-Ghozi was arrested in Manila in January 2002.

In February 2003, Singapore's Internal Security Department revealed that it had found emails and letters linking Maidin, the leader of the Singapore JI operation, with Mullah Omar, Mohammed Atta, and Osama bin Laden in Kabul.[70] These contacts dated from 1999. A sophisticated attempt to damage the fraught bilateral relations with Malaysia informed the strategic thinking of the Singapore plot. The aim was to create conflict between the two neighbors and thus destabilize the regional order that the Association of South East Asian Nations (ASEAN), formed in 1967, had crafted after the European colonial powers eventually departed the region.

Mohammed Mansoor Jabarah, a 19-year-old Kuwaiti with Canadian citizenship who had met with bin Laden on at least four occasions, financed the operation and provided its link to al-Qaeda.[71] Jabarah escaped to Malaysia in December 2001. Subsequently, Khalid

Sheikh Mohammed sent Jabarah to organize new missions with Hambali. In January 2002 Jabarah met with Hambali, Omar al-Faruq, the al-Qaeda representative in Southeast Asia,[72] and he met Mukhlas and Noordin Top in Southern Thailand. Here they agreed on a campaign to attack soft targets with Western links like the Kuta Beach resort in Bali.[73] Jabarah provided $US 150,000 for the Bali operation. Hambali delegated the planning and execution of this mission to Mukhlas.[74] Mukhlas chose Imam Samudra from a Persis family in West Java to lead the Bali operation, and he recruited a hard core of al-Mukmin graduates. Azahari Hussin directed Ali Imron, Amrozi, Mubarok, Sarjiyo, Umar Patek, and Dul Matin to construct the bombs responsible for the attack on Paddy's Bar on October 12, 2002.[75] Ultimately, it was the tight structure, long-term strategic planning, and rigidity of the ideological mission that was central to the success of the operation.

After Bali

IN PIECING TOGETHER THE EVOLVING RELATIONSHIP BETWEEN JI, ABU SAYYAF, AND al-Qaeda between 1985 and 2002, it is clear that regional intelligence and police services exhibited a marked degree of complacency about the nature and threat they posed to regional security. For example, Jabarah was detained in March 2002 and Faruq was arrested in August 2002. An FBI report from their interrogations was made available to Australian and regional intelligence agencies in August 2002.[76] Yet, even after the Bali bombs, Australian police and intelligence still officially denied any connection between JI and al-Qaeda. In January 2003, Australian police sources even maintained that "there [was] nothing concrete to link al-Qaeda to the [Bali] bombings."[77] Eventually, in February it was officially but somewhat obscurely announced that "until the events of October 12, [JI was] an unknown quantity."[78]

In many ways, the scale of the intelligence failure across the region reflected a wider inter-governmental complacency towards the spread of Islamist extremism prior to the Bali bombing. The region consistently underestimated the nature and extent of the threat. Thus, regional scholar bureaucrats like Jusuf Wanandi of the Center for Strategic and International Studies in Jakarta maintained that "attention to such groups as Laskar Jihad has been overblown. They are rather noisy groups, but small and marginal."[79] Such views found their echo in Australian assessments where security analysts claimed barely a week before the Bali attack that "the tendency is still to overplay [the terror] threat."[80]

Given the protoplasmic character of al-Qaeda, with JI sleeper cells extending even to Australia, the threat remained pervasive between 2002 and 2009. Before the Bali attack, ASEAN had set up a number of discussion forums to look into the issue of extremism in the region. However, the association was often divided by outlook amongst its members and even failed to agree on an acceptable definition of terrorism.[81]

After the Bali bombing, ASEAN nations increased low-level intelligence cooperation. Nevertheless, the Association remained hamstrung in dealing with the Southeast Asian terror network. This thwarting of cooperation was a result of the association's commitment to the principle of non-interference in the internal affairs of member states.[82] As a consequence, some ASEAN states, along with regional commentary more generally, continued to exhibit a degree of ambivalence toward the global interconnectedness of militant Islamism and its terror links between 2002 and 2005.[83] In Indonesia in the aftermath of the authoritarian New Order, the Presidency of Megawati Sukarnoputri (2001-2004) officially discounted links between regional Islamism and globalizing transnational terror—despite mounting evidence to the contrary. Interestingly, the 35-page indictment of the Bali night club bomber, Amrozi, did not refer once to his membership in JI.[84] Additionally, the subsequent indictment of JI emir Bashir made no mention of his links to al-Qaeda.[85] Bashir was arraigned on charges of trying to topple Indonesia's secular government, assassinate President Megawati, and establish an Islamic state. Of course, Bashir dismissed all the charges against him as a CIA plot and threatened then-U.S. President Bush with "punishment by Allah."[86]

Moreover, the arrest of the Bali bombers by no means rendered JI redundant. Indeed, the core of JI's militant faction remained at large. Bomb attacks in May 2003 on Jakarta airport and in the Philippines demonstrated JI's continuing terror capability, and this was reinforced by the attack on the Marriott hotel on August 5 in which a dozen people died. The bombing of the Australian embassy in Jakarta in September 2004, the second attack on Bali in October 2005 in which 23 died, and the martyrdom attack on the Marriott and Ritz-Carlton hotels in the Mega Kuningan business district of Jakarta in July 2009 that killed 9 people substantiated the continuing capacity of the group to conduct operations. Its protean character, combined with the fact that al-Qaeda operated as a global conduit for anti-Western resentment, meant that it had become more dangerously elusive after 2002.

Indeed, a study by Sidney Jones in 2003 suggested that JI was a much larger organization than previously suspected, "with a depth of leadership that [gave] it a regenerative capacity."[87] In August 2003, Australian Federal Police Commissioner Mick Keelty maintained that JI would not be defeated while the Indonesian government permitted pesantren like al-Mukmin to recruit future generations for the jihadist cause. Somewhat predictably, the Indonesian Foreign Minister Hassan Wirayuda dismissed Keelty's observations as "fortune teller's talk" and an intolerable intrusion into Indonesian domestic politics.[88]

However, Commissioner Keelty's prophecies were confirmed when in September 2003 a Jakarta court convicted Abu Bakar Bashir of subversion rather than treason and sentenced him to only four years in prison. The court found insufficient evidence to prove that he was the leader of JI or that he conspired in the planning of terrorist operations. He was released from jail in 2006 and continued to preside over his boarding school at Pondok Ngruki near Solo in Central Java.

In fact, Bashir was only rearrested and accused of treason after the discovery and disruption of a hitherto unsuspected terror cell, "al-Qaeda in Aceh," in February 2010, which had links to both the more militant elements in JI like Dul Matin and Nordin Top as well as to Bashir who allegedly raised $150,000 AU for the group. The Aceh cell was comprised of both Indonesian activists as well as "militants who had ties to both the Middle East and the Philippines."[89] According to Indonesian counterterrorism reports, the group had planned to not only assassinate Indonesian President Susilo Bambang Yudhoyono but also to mount a Mumbai-style attack in Jakarta on Independence Day (August 17, 2010).[90] Indonesian authorities detained over 100 more people in connection with the February raid. Despite its disruption after 2002, the picture that emerged in light of these events was that JI still retained its hierarchy of accountability and that Bashir functioned as far more than a spiritual leader of the organization. It also appeared from this recent investigation that JI had a capacity for renewal that most commentators had underestimated—not least because what was being planned in Aceh was a full-scale training camp for jihad.[91]

In this context of regional denial and misunderstanding of the resilient character of JI, it should be further noted that in 2003 the Thai government threatened to prosecute any foreign journalist who alleged that senior al-Qaeda operatives like Hambali had ever met in the Muslim-populated Thai south to coordinate attacks across the region—despite well-informed reports that this was indeed the case.[92] In June however, then-Thai Prime Minister Thaksin Shinawatra, who had previously derided travel warnings against his country, somewhat lost face when Thai police uncovered a JI cell actively planning suicide bomb attacks on Western embassies in Bangkok. Hambali's arrest in the former Thai capital of Ayodhaya in August 2003 augmented the Thai government's embarrassment.

In April/May 2010, it was revealed that JI members ran a school complex in Phnom Penh, Cambodia and had opened a new training camp in southern Mindanao that gave diplomas to its graduates. Once more, this indicated the adaptive qualities of the organization. The largely unregulated borderland region that includes parts of Mindanao (islands in the Sulu Sea), the Malaysian state of Sabah, and northern Indonesia continues to offer sanctuary to those opposed to the secular governments of the region. Moreover, despite continued harrying by the Philippine military and police, the Abu Sayyaf threat remained serious enough to prompt the Philippine government to postpone an ASEAN Ministers meeting and East Asian Summit planned for Cebu in November 2006. Finally, as noted above, in 2010, Indonesian Special Forces disrupted an unsuspected jihadist training camp in Aceh organized by Tanzim al-Qaeda Indonesia dari Serambi Makkah, a purported breakaway faction of JI.

Degrading and Dismantling JI

DESPITE THE RECOGNITION OF JI'S CONTINUING PRESENCE, NEVERTHELESS WHEN the usual lack of coordination among the internal security apparatuses of regional states was overcome and the traditionally fragmented minds of the ASEAN states were concentrated, Southeast Asian states became able to expose and disrupt JI and its transnational connections—particularly if they utilized Australian and U.S. expertise. After October 2002, the Indonesian police arrested 34 members of the JI group whose existence the government officially doubted until 2005. While Bashir received a light sentence, Amrozi, Imam Samudra, and Ali Imron were found guilty and sentenced to death in Denpasar, Bali in August 2003 for securing the explosives and the car for the Bali nightclub bombings.

Furthermore, after the second Bali bombing and the election of new President Susilo Bambang Yudhoyono in 2004, the Indonesian police developed the resolve and capacity to dismantle the JI network with the assistance of the Australian Federal Police and the U.S. armed forces. After 2004, the Indonesian police received a clear mandate to excise, by force if necessary, the most militant JI group, Mantiqi 1. The police paramilitary unit *Brimob* (Brigade Mobile) and particularly its second anti-terror regiment *Gegana*—together with the U.S.-trained and funded special forces group, *Detasemen Khusus* or *Desus 88* (Detachment 88), which was operational by 2005—subsequently harried the militant wing of JI across the archipelago. In 2005, *Desus 88* raided a house in Malang East Java and killed Azahari Hussin, the bomb maker and coordinator responsible for the Bali, Marriott Hotel and Australian embassy attacks with Noordin Top. In January 2007, *Desus 88* engaged in an operation in Poso, Sulawesi where ten jihadists died in a gunfight. Following these raids, inter-communal violence in Sulawesi declined dramatically. The counterinsurgency achieved another notable coup in June 2007 with the arrest of Abu Dujana, the head of JI's military wing, together with the new supreme leader of JI, Zarkasih. The arrests of Dujana and Zarkasih severely disrupted the post-Bali organization of JI.

Therefore, by 2007, the JI network responsible for the Bali bombing had been significantly degraded. Hambali, Mukhlas, Faiz Bafana, Abu Jibril, Abu Rusdan, and the Bali bombers were all in jail, while Azahari Hussin and Fathur Rahman al-Ghozi were dead. The remnant of JI's military hard core—Noordin Top, Umar Patek, and Dul Matin—remained, albeit briefly, in the Southern Philippines where they resumed their long-standing ties with the Abu Sayyaf Group. In the course of 2007, JI further fragmented. Noordin Top, the charismatic "moneyman" and acknowledged link to al-Qaeda, along with the remnant of Mantiqi 1, seemingly broke from Bashir and the political leadership of JI and declared his leadership of a new group, the *Tanzim al-Qaeda* (or *Tanzim Qaedat al-Jihad*, Organization for the Basis of Jihad). Subsequently, the faction led by Top conducted the July 2009 attack on the Jakarta Ritz-Carlton and Marriott hotels. This, however, was to be the group's apogee. Two months later Top was dead. Detachment 88 officers killed him in a shoot-out at a house in Solo, Central Java. Later, in March 2010, Detachment 88 officers shot and killed "Indonesia's most wanted man," Dul Matin, outside an Internet cafe on the outskirts of Jakarta, acting on information received from the arrest of JI sympathizers in Aceh.[93] This left Umar Patek, the last major figure of the Bali generation of bombers, isolated and on the run. The Pakistan ISI eventually detained Patek in Abbotabad in January 2011. He was subsequently extradited to Indonesia in August. *Tanzim Qaedat al-Jihad* was effectively neutralized after the February raid on their Aceh training camp.

In the Philippines, the police and military continued their protracted campaign against Abu Sayyaf and related militias in Mindanao. The police killed Khadaffy Janjalani in 2006 and his successor, Abu Suleiman, in January 2007. Romeo Ricardo, chief of police intelligence, maintained that Khadaffy and Suleiman had been the main contacts both for Middle Eastern donors and for JI.

In Malaysia, which had hosted both Zacarias Moussaoui and a number of late participants in the events of 9/11, government security forces interned 62 members of the JI-affiliated KMM. Those arrested included the alleged leader of the KMM, Nik Adli Abdul Aziz, whose father was Nik Aziz Nik Mat, the spiritual head of the Malaysian Islamic opposition party (PAS) and the former Premier of the state of Kelantan. Malaysian police also interned college lecturer Wan bin Wan Mat who was responsible for transferring money to Imam Samudra for the Bali attack and to the group's spiritual leader, Abu Jibril. By Indonesia taking more forceful action both domestically and regionally after 2004—even cooperating with Singaporean authorities to arrest the head of the Singapore branch of JI and participating in joint operations with the Australian Federal Police to dismantle JI's military wing—it negated any integrated capacity for Islamist groupings to mount terror attacks across the region. Moreover, the arrests of Omar al Faruq in August 2002, the 9/11 mastermind Khalid Sheikh Mohammed in March 2003, and JI chief strategist Hambali by U.S. special forces in Thailand in August 2003 further restricted links between JI and al-Qaeda's already disrupted military council and further denuded its operational effectiveness.

In other words, coordinated counter-terror targeting and decapitating of key network hubs proved remarkably effective at disrupting the organization. JI's militant faction's commitment to tactical bombings, which had killed more Indonesians than *kafir* Westerners, further facilitated what Detachment 88 Commander Tito M. Karnavian termed, "the carrot and stick" approach of Indonesia's elite paramilitary police:[94] Simply, attacks on Indonesians after 2003 alienated the majority of moderate Muslims.

The Southeast Asian
Counter-Ideology Campaigns

AT THE SAME TIME, AS MORE EFFECTIVE REGIONAL POLICING, INTELLIGENCE, AND counterinsurgency operations disrupted JI and its links with KMM, Abu Sayyaf, and al-Qaeda, a number of regional governments also launched initiatives to counter the ideology espoused by JI and its affiliates in the MMI. Although regional governments have disrupted jihad in Indonesia and Malaysia, this observation is not unimportant because the democratic transition in Indonesia since 1999 and the increasing openness of Malaysian politics since 2004 has provided an opening for Islamism to advance its ideology via non-violent political means. Furthermore, the discovery of the Aceh cell and its continuing transnational links revealed in February 2010 that JI possessed resilience and capacity for recruitment. The continuing threat from jihadist violence should not be underestimated for these reasons.

Significantly, the more astute and pragmatic figures in JI have recognized and exploited the opportunity offered by the prospect of democratic openings in Indonesia. Since 2007, the long-serving emir of JI, Bashir, has promoted a political Islamist agenda, while at the same time covertly supporting and subsidizing the production of violence by groups like "al-Qaeda in Aceh." His message of transforming the political state into an Islamic one continued to converge with that of Islamist political parties like the *Partai Keadilan Sejahtera* (PKS, Prosperous Justice Party) and *Hizb ut-Tahrir*. The latter operated both regionally and transnationally to advance the caliphate. But unlike JI, PKS eschewed active and physical jihad—at least officially.

Consequently, to confront the ideological appeal of jihadism, a number of regional governments have revived or modified strategies to sustain internal cohesion and national resilience that had been developed in the immediate aftermath of colonialism. This is not without interest given that Southeast Asian states like Malaysia, Singapore, and Indonesia had been the focus of classical counterinsurgency practice in the 1950s and 1960s. Significantly, in the Cold War period it was these insecure new states that paid conspicuous attention to nation building and internal resilience in the face of a variety of external and internal threats. Indonesia, for instance, evolved its secular identity of unity in diversity via the national ideology of *Pancasila*. After race riots in 1969, Malaysia devised its national pillars or *Rukun Negara*. Meantime, Singapore developed a strategy of "total defense," a crucial dimension of which required a psychological defense designed to reinforce loyalty to and trust in government.[95]

Furthermore, in attending to national resilience and internal security, these states have increasingly recognized that the threat posed by violent extremism is not only one of inadequate public policy alone, but it is also of ideological motivation and recruitment. As Rohan Gunaratna of Nanyang Technological University, Singapore, observes, "ideology not poverty or illiteracy" is "the key driver of politically motivated violence."[96] In this statement, he merely asserts the view not only of the Singapore government but also of the moderate Muslim ruling parties in Indonesia and Malaysia. In Malaysia, the former Prime Minister Abdullah Badawi promoted a civilizational Islam, or Islam *Hadhari,* which emphasized Islamic tolerance, market friendliness, and pluralism. Current Prime Minister Najib endorses a "One Malaysia" policy to overcome racial and religious tension. This policy, combined with internal security legislation dating from the Malaya Emergency period between 1948 and 1960 that aims to interdict those suspected of membership in radical Islamist groups, has succeeded in curtailing Islamist inspired violence in Malaysia.

Analogously, in Indonesia the Wahid Institute (named for the late President Wahid) promotes a moderate Muslim voice that emphasizes Islam as a moral and social teaching rather than a political ideology. *Nahdlatul Ulama*, the largest Muslim organization in the world, promotes this thinking across the archipelago. Wahid's critique of radical Islamist ideas also promotes this thinking. He contended that while radical Islam presented a growing challenge, *Nahdlatul* nevertheless had the resources and the energy to combat it. As he pointed out, "every Saturday morning I have a broadcast of one hour over the radio regarding religious issues. Now [in 2007] it reaches 10 million listeners, while before [2002] it was only half a million. This shows our peaceful message is heard now more than ever."[97] Moderate teaching, together with the Indonesian government and paramilitary police's increasingly combative approach to JI militancy, has significantly degraded, though not destroyed, JI's capacity to act as a violently subversive organization. As *Desus 88* commander Karnavian declared, "the carrot and stick approach" to jihad has had notable success in fragmenting the hard core from its support base. This tactic was further facilitated by the inept targeting of the militant JI faction in their post-2002 bombing campaign.[98]

Therefore, the strategies adopted by Southeast Asian states emphasize a central awareness of al-Qaeda's ideology and the capacity to address it—or more precisely, to "de-sacralize" its appeal and undermine its legitimacy. It could be argued that this awareness is as important in combating the jihadist enterprise as it is to disrupting its organizational hubs. Thus, as a 2006 report on *Terrorism in Southeast Asia* observed, "weaning the mainstream Muslims away from [Islamist] influence through political concessions, amnesties, or other personal initiatives" is not enough. Instead, "the best chances for success [are] [sic] to engage them in dialogue, show them how they are being manipulated by perverted or corrupt interpretations of the religious texts, and to convince them that there could be better alternatives to acts of violence."[99] Outlining what this entails in terms of counter-ideological practice, Gunaratna notes that until recently "the ideological or intellectual battle has been overlooked," especially by those counterinsurgency experts such as David Kilcullen who maintain that the counter-ideological campaign is a second-order concern given that Islamist thought possesses "little functional relationship with violence."[100] In the words of Gunaratna, one consequence of such views is that "there has been no effort to ideologically target al Qaeda, JI, and other comparable groups that apply religious justification to legitimate and authenticate their terrorist activities."[101]

To address this view, Singapore, and the region more generally, adopted a more proactive strategy (if somewhat belatedly). The Singapore government worked within an established framework to sustain national resilience and maintain harmony within its diverse communities and acted in conjunction with the moderate Muslim community, in the words of the former Prime Minister Goh Chok Tong, "to root out extremists and radical teaching."[102] In this effort, Deputy Minister for Home Affairs Wong Kan Seng argued, "the government cannot deal with the terrorist ideology by changing the minds of the detainees who have been poisoned. This has to be done by the religious teachers and scholars themselves."[103] Thus, in order to combat the "deviant ideology," the government-linked Muslim community organizations must address the distortions present in JI ideology as well as counsel Singapore's 31 JI members detained under the state's draconic Internal Security Act since 2002.[104] After 2003 in particular, the Muslim Religious Council of Singapore established a register of religious teachers (*asatizah*) as part of a "comprehensive regulatory system."[105] This system also involves prominent Singaporean Muslim clerics counseling jihadists as well as engaging directly with their ideology. Muslim scholars Ustaz Haji ali Haji Mohamed and Ustaz Haji Mohamed Hasbi bin Feisal Hassan, President of the Singapore Islamic Scholars and Religious Teachers Association, became the core personnel of the Religious Rehabilitation Group (RRG) devoted to correcting the misconceived ideology held by JI detainees and disseminated its corrections across the Muslim community.[106] The RRG undertakes counseling of those who have been radicalized. Since 2005, the RRG has successfully rehabilitated 26 former JI sympathizers who have been released back into the community, albeit on restriction orders. In the Southeast Asian context, therefore, security analysts like Noor Huda Ismail consider ideological rehabilitation crucial "because it tackles the heart of the problem, a radical reinterpretation of Islamic teachings."[107]

Apart from their counseling program, *asatizah* like Muhammad Hassan also play an active role in confuting Islamist writings and their justifications for jihadist violence. Hassan, like Wahid in Indonesia, addressed the questionable use of the Koran to defend the jihadist recourse to violence. Hassan notably undertook a detailed criticism of Bali bomber Imam Samudra's best seller *Aku Melawan Teroris* (I Fight Terrorists, 2004). Samudra defended the Bali bombing in 2002 on the grounds that Muslim lands needed defense against the infidel crusade. Jihad, moreover, is not only necessary but constitutes a personal obligation (*fardhu ain*) for the true as opposed to the fake or chocolate Muslim.

By contrast, Hassan drew upon Islamic theology to show that Samudra's personal obligation to jihad negated the concept of rightful authority in Islam and that his generalization about the necessity of jihad against non-believers is one that no established Muslim scholarship sustains. Ultimately, Hassan demonstrated that Samudra's thinking tends to conspiracy theory rather than to faith.

Significantly, therefore, the governments of Indonesia, Singapore, and Malaysia have recognized since 2002 that "no counter ideology work can succeed and no correct alternative ideas can be offered, unless a clear and accurate understanding of the opposing ideology held by jihadists is established."[108] As Hassan concludes, "the problem of violent extremism is twofold: misinterpretation of the text and the opportunity and context that provide for such misinterpretation."[109]

Conclusion

THIS GENEALOGY OF ISLAMIST-INSPIRED GROUPS IN SOUTHEAST ASIA DEMONSTRATES both the long-term thinking and planning of al-Qaeda and its protean and diffuse character. These characteristics enabled the movement to connect with Islamist organizations as far afield as Indonesia, Malaysia, the Philippines, and Singapore, interact with them, finance them, and subordinate them to achieve the movement's strategic goals. Its capacity to draw disparate radical groups together, to coordinate their ideology and practice through collaboration and exchange, and to broaden the reach of these groups from local to national to regional and beyond, contrasts with the partial understandings of the threat initially exhibited by regional intelligence agencies and commentators that were limited by national horizons and bureaucratic or government-determined agendas.

While JI has been significantly degraded from being an effective regional organization, it has nevertheless succeeded in making its ideology both widely available and increasingly attractive to Southeast Asian Muslims confronted by the uncertainty of regional politics and the anxiety generated by globalization. As the Jakarta hotel bombings of July 2009 and the disruption of a training camp in Aceh in early 2010 demonstrate, JI's continuing appeal to a new generation of radicals remains potent, despite the increasingly fragmented character of its extremist faction. In other words, the survival of the organization is not necessarily central to the continuation of the threat but the dissemination of the ideology and the polymorphous violence it strategically embraces is central to its continuation. This evolution and development evidently refutes the thesis of Jessica Stern, Marc Sageman, David Kilcullen, and others who downplay religious motivation in jihadist activism. Ultimately, the mission is not flexible and its promulgation requires commitment, sacrifice, and a determined obduracy. These are demonstrated in the propensity for martyrdom of not only foot soldiers like the Bali bombers but also of regional "hubs"—to use Sageman's somewhat clumsy term—like Noordin Top and Dul Matin.

Moreover, the success of the Indonesian, Malaysian, and Singaporean authorities in countermanding the organization demonstrates the importance of a counter-ideological campaign that seeks to de-sacralize the appeal to violence in the name of religion. This uncompromising response, further reinforced by a commitment to eradicate or decapitate the hardcore leadership, has proved highly effective, despite the cavils of Western experts like Audrey Kurth Cronin who prefer negotiation and imprisonment.

In this assessment of the complex linkages binding and sustaining Islamist groupings in Southeast Asia, we have demonstrated that understanding organizational evolution and "informal networks" is useful as an analytical tool to aid comprehension of how jihadist groups form, develop, mutate, and spread. However, making the organizational structure the central explanatory variable for jihadist activity, as many contemporary commentators do, confuses ends and means.

Ultimately, informal networks are the means, not the ends, of jihadist actions. Complex networking is instrumental to the spread of Islamist ideology. The contention is validated when we examine the motives for broadening the web of jihadist activism throughout Southeast Asia during the first decade of the twentieth century and its continuing resilience today. This conclusion is reinforced by the official attitudes and actions of the states of Southeast Asia that have put a premium on confronting the ideological motivation for jihad as the cornerstone of their counterterror policy and which, as we have shown, have done much to degrade the effectiveness of the networking that sustains groups like JI.

Contrary to organizational approaches, then, a case study of Southeast Asian jihadist militancy suggests that ideology remains the crucial variable involved in the motivation, maintenance, and indeed organization of Islamist groups—while countering them necessitates a judicious blend of force and counter radicalization strategies. Maintaining political stability in Southeast Asia requires the continuation of this broad national security strategy that attempts not only to interdict violent jihadist conspiracies but also prudently attends to the deracinating consequences of new political religions. This, moreover, constitutes a template for designing strategies that could also be useful in societies beyond Southeast Asia, including Europe and North America.

NOTES

1. See "Alien Arrests Bid to Flush Out 'Sleepers'," *Bangkok Post*, March 11, 2002; Reme Ahmad, "KL Arrests 23 Islamic Militants in Swoop," *Straits Times*, January 5, 2002.

2. See, for example, Justin Magouirk, Scott Atran and Marc Sageman "Connecting Terrorist Networks" *Studies in Conflict and Terrorism*, Vol. 31, No. 1 (2008), pp. 1-16.

3. See David Martin Jones and M.L.R. Smith, "The Perils of Hyper-Vigilance: The War on Terrorism and the Surveillance State in Southeast Asia," *Intelligence and National Security*, Vol. 17, No. 4 (Winter 2002), pp. 31-54.

4. An indication of the inaccurate comprehension of al-Qaeda's future threat potential was illustrated by Robert Fisk, "Anti-Soviet Warrior Puts His Army on the Road to Peace," *The Independent*, December 6, 1993. It was Fisk's opinion that the "Saudi businessman who recruited mujahideen now used them for large-scale building projects in Sudan."

5. See Sayyid Qutb, *Islam: The Religion of the Future* (Kuwait: International Islamic Federation of Students, 1971); and Elie Kedourie, *Democracy and Arab Political Culture* (London: Frank Cass, 1994), pp. 94-100.

6. Abdullah Azzam was a Jordanian-Palestinian scholar and a Muslim Brotherhood radical. He studied Islamic law at Cairo's Al-Azhar University. Inspired by the prospect of being able to put the principles of Islamic resistance into practice, he was one of the first Arabs to leave for Afghanistan to fight the Soviet occupation after 1979. In 1980 he founded *Maktab al-Khidmat lil-Mujahideen al-Arab* (MaK) (the general translation is the "College that Serves the Arab Warriors" but it is often rendered in English as the Afghan Service Office), in Peshawar, Pakistan. MaK formed one of the umbrella groups of the foreign fighters of the Afghan Mujahideen and was part of the Muslim World League. It was here along the Afghanistan-Pakistan border that Osama bin Laden, the Islamicized scion of a wealthy Saudi family, first encountered Azzam. Azzam became Osama's ideological guru. Osama bankrolled MaK and honored Azzam with the appendage the "Emir of Jihad." The recruitment of Arab fighters for the Afghan struggle meant that from early on MaK became heavily infiltrated by groups like the Egyptian *al Gamma al Islamiyya*, the Palestinian Hamas and the Algerian *Groupe Islamique Armée*. It was MaK that was to form the nucleus of later ideas about developing a transnational jihad and which was to evolve into the entity known as *al-Qaeda*. It is claimed that Azzam and Osama were to fall out over the future direction of the MaK, though precisely over what seems to be a matter of debate. Some say Azzam had less commitment to global jihad. Other accounts suggest both men got caught up in Afghan tribal politics with Azzam supporting Ahmed Shah Massoud's Northern Alliance while Osama supported the Taliban. Evidently though, while in Afghanistan Osama developed far more sympathy for the views of the militant Egyptian surgeon Dr Ayman al-Zawahiri (and later leader of the *al Gamma al Islamiyya*) who proclaimed that "Afghanistan should be a platform for the liberation of the entire Muslim world." Azzam was assassinated in a car bomb in Peshawar, in September 1989, which, fortuitously or not, permitted the hard-line elements within the *Maktab al-Khidmat* like al-Zawahri and Osama himself to predominate. See Fiona Symons, "Analysis: The Roots of Jihad," *BBC News*, February 16, 2003, at
http://news.bbc.co.uk/1/hi/world/middle_east/1603178.stm (accessed October 28, 2004); Mohamad Bazi, "Bin Laden's 'Logistical Mastermind'," *New York Newsday*, September 21, 2001; Pierre Conesa, "Al-Qaida, The Sect," Le Monde Diplomatique, January 2002 at

http://mondediplo.com/2002/01/07sect (accessed October 28, 2004); and, "Al-Qaeda (The Base)," Center for Defense Information (Washington, DC), December 20, 2002.

7. See Richard Engel, "Inside Al-Qaeda: A Window into the World of Militant Islam and the Afghan Alumni," *Jane's International Security*, September 28, 2001, republished at *Free Republic*. http://www.freerepublic.com/focus/f-news/559098/posts (accessed February 28, 2011).

8. Ibid.

9. Jessica Stern and Amit Modi, "Producing Terror: Organizational Dynamics of Survival," in Thomas J. Biersteker and Sue E. Eckert (eds.), *Countering the Financing of Terrorism* (London: Routledge, 2008), p. 20.

10. Ibid., p. 21.

11. Audrey Kurth Cronin, *How Terrorism Ends: Understanding the Demise and Decline of Terrorism Campaigns* (Princeton, NJ: Princeton University Press, 2009) p. 171.

12. Ibid., p. 172.

13. Marc Sageman, *Understanding Terror Networks* (Philadelphia: University of Pennsylvania Press, 2004), p. 137.

14. Ibid., p. 40.

15. Ibid., p. 126.

16. Max Abrahms, "What Terrorists Really Want: Terrorist Motives and Counterterrorism Strategy," *International Security*, Vol. 32, No. 4, (Spring 2008), p. 103.

17. It is sometimes queried whether it is correct to say that al-Qaeda existed in the 1980s. It is uncertain when the grouping actually came into being, though 1989 is often stated as the year of its formation. However, what we now call *al-Qaeda* is in fact simply the name given to the later evolution of the MaK. There is even evidence to suggest that "al-Qaeda" is not self-given, but was merely the name of a file found on Osama bin Laden's personal computer listing members and contacts within the MaK. Thus, the appendage "al-Qaeda" appears to have been coined by the U.S. authorities as convenient shorthand to describe the loose, if rather complex, arrangements of a network based on MaK's membership. See "Al-Qaeda's Origins and Links," *BBC News*, July 20, 2004 at http://news.bbc.co.uk/1/hi/world/south_asia/1670089.stm (accessed October 2, 2004); "Blowback," *Jane's Intelligence Review*, July 26, 2001 (accessed October 7, 2004). See also Rohan Gunaratna, "The al-Qaeda Threat and the International Response," in David Martin Jones (ed.), *Globalisation and the New Terror : The Asia Pacific Dimension* (London: Edward Elgar, 2004).

18. *Jemaah Islamiah* is the Malay and Indonesian translation of the Arabic *al Jemmat* or the Egyptian *al Gamma*, which denotes either a group or community. *Islamiah*, sometimes spelt *Islamiyah* in its Indonesian variant, is the Arabic *Islami* or the adjectival form of the noun Islam.

19. See Robert Hefner, *Civil Islam* (Princeton, NJ: Princeton University Press, 2000), esp. chapter 1.

20. See Greg Barton, *Jemaah Islamiyah: Radical Islamism in Indonesia* (Singapore: National University of Singapore Press, 2005), p. 45.

21. Author interview with Abdurrahman Wahid (Gus Dur), PNU office, Central Jakarta, June 4, 2007.

22. An ideology of resistance by poor workers and rural dwellers against the rich, ruling elite: Marhaen being the name of an Indonesian farmer who was content with his simple life.

23. See Asia Watch, *Human Rights in Indonesia and East Timor* (New York: Asia Watch, 1989), pp. 76-85.

24. See "Hambali Plotted Terror Campaign," *The Star* (Malaysia), January 1, 2003.

25. International Crisis Group, "Al-Qaeda in Southeast Asia: The Case of the 'Ngruki Network' in Indonesia," August 8, 2002, reissued January 10, 2003, at http://www.crisisgroup.org/en/regions/asia/southeast-asia/indonesia/B020-al-qaeda-in-southeast-asia-the-case-of-the-ngruki-network-in-indonesia-corrected-on-10-January-2003.aspx (accessed August 30, 2003).

26. The five principles are: belief in one god; a civilized community; national unity; guided democracy and social justice.

27. Greg Barton, *Jemaah Islamiyah*, p. 114; and Magouirk, Atran, and Sageman, "Connecting Terror Networks," p. 9.

28. Rohan Gunaratna, "Ideology in Terrorism and Counter Terrorism: Lesson from combating Al Qaeda and al-Jamaah al-Islamiyyah in Southeast Asia," in Abdul Halim Bin Kader (ed.), *Fighting Terrorism: The Singapore Dimension* (Singapore Tamaan Bacaan, 2007), pp. 84-85.

29. "Hambali: SE Asia's Most Wanted," BBC News/Asia-Pacific, October 21, 2002, at http://news.bbc.co.uk/1/low/world/asia-pacific/2346225.htm (accessed February 6, 2004).

30. Abu Walid al-Masri (b. 1945) was an Arab volunteer for the Afghan Mujahideen during the Soviet occupation and is regarded as a key influence over the evolution of al-Qaeda.

31. Dan Murphy, "Man 'Most Wanted' in Indonesia," *Christian Science Monitor*, April 30, 2002.

32. See David Martin Jones and M.L.R. Smith, "Identity Politics in Southeast Asia," *Jane's Intelligence Review*, Vol. 12, No. 11 (November 2000), pp. 44-45. Malaysia has hosted at least thirteen radical groups that sought to reform the state along Islamist lines since the formation of the federation in 1963. From the *Tentera Sabilullah* (Holy War Army) that operated out of Kedah down to the *Kumpulan Persaudaraan Ilmu dalam Al-Maunah* (Brotherhood of Al-Maunah Inner Power) that successfully raided an army base in Perak in 2000. Malaysian Islam has demonstrated a neglected and albeit minority avocation for jihadism. The *Kumpulan Militan* or *Kumpulan Mujahideen Malaysia* clearly fits in this tradition. See Mohammed Mizan Aslam, "The Thirteen Radical Groups: Preliminary Research in Understanding the Evolution of Islamist Militancy in Malaysia," *JATI—Journal of Southeast Asian Studies*, Vol. 14, No. 1 (December 2009), pp. 145-161.

See also Kumpulan Mujahidin Malaysia (KMM), Federation of American Scientists, at http://www.fas.org/irp/world/para/kmm.htm (accessed May 11, 2010).

33. See Greg Barton, "An Islamist North Australia: Al Qaeda's Vision," *The Age*, October 30, 2002.

34. Barton, *Jemaah Islamiyah*, pp. 56-57.

35. International Crisis Group, "Al-Qaeda in Southeast Asia."

36. Dan Murphy, "Al Qaeda's Asian 'Quartermaster'," *Christian Science Monitor*, February 12, 2002.

37. See "Tentacles of Terror," *The Bulletin*, February 13, 2002 and David Martin Jones and M.L.R. Smith, "The Strange Death of the ASEAN Way," *Australian Financial Review*, April 12, 2002.

38. See "Bush Backs Independent 9-11 Probe," CBSNews.com, September 20, 2002, at http://www.cbsnews.com/stories/2002/09/24/attack/main523156.shtml (accessed November 21, 2002) and "The FBI's Hijacker List," CBSNews.com, September 27, 2001, at http://www.cbsnews.com/stories/2001/09/14/archive/main311329.shtml?tag=mncol;lst;1 (accessed November 27, 2002).

39. Mark Fineman and Bob Drogin, "Indonesian Cleric Had Role in Skyjackings, Officials Say," *Los Angeles Times*, February 2, 2002.

40. *Straits Times*, January 10, 2003.

41. Farah Abdul Rahim, "White Paper Sheds Light on Singapore JI Indoctrination Process," Channel News Asia.com, January 9, 2003, at http://www.channelnewsasia.com/stories/singaporelocalnews/view/29264/1/.html (accessed March 12, 2004).

42. See Office of Public Affairs (Washington, DC), "Statement by the Treasury Department Regarding Today's Designation of Two Leaders of Jemaah Islamiyah," January 24, 2003, KD-3796.

43. Jack Roche, the Australian former JI member, observed this JI practice in an interview with Sally

Neighbour. See Sally Neighbour, "Indonesia Terror Optimism Premature," *Weekend Australian*, August 14-15, 2010.

44. "The Bali Bomber's Network of Terror," BBC News/Asia-Pacific, August 6, 2003 at http://news.bbc.co.uk/2/hi/asia-pacific/2499193.stm (accessed March 15, 2004).

45. See Magouirk, Atran and Sageman, "Connecting Terrorist Networks," pp. 1-16.

46. The US State Department's *Patterns of Global Terrorism 2002* formally lists the Abu Sayyaf Group as having broken away from the MNLF in the early 1990s under Abdurajak Abubakar Janjalani http://www.state.gov/s/ct/rls/crt/2002/ (accessed June 18, 2003), although this is questioned by other analysts who argue that it evolved somewhat more independently based on the Tausug ethnic group. See also Federation of American Scientists, at http://www.fas.org/irp/world/para/Abu Sayyaf.htm (accessed June 19, 2004). For a more concerted examination of the general development of Moro separatism see Peter Gowing, *Muslim Filipinos* (Manila: Solidaridad, 1974) and W.K. Che Man, *Muslim Separatism: The Moros of the Philippines and the Malays of Southern Thailand* (Oxford: Oxford University Press, 1990), chapter 1.

47. *Manila Times*, November 1, 2002.

48. *The Guardian*, September 23, 2001.

49. Lira Dalangin, "MILF: Camp Abubakar Upland Military's Next Goal," *Newsbreak* (Philippines), February 17, 2003 at http://www.inq7.net/brk/2003/feb/17/brkpol_4-1.htm (accessed June 23, 2004).

50. See C.C. Hidalgo, "Camp Abubakar: A Symbol of Muslim Pride," Codewan.com (Philippines), May 17, 2000, at http://www.codewan.com.ph/CyberDyaryo/features/f2000_0515_01.htm (accessed June 19, 2004).

51. Republic of Philippines Directorate for Intelligence, "Reference Folder on International Terrorism," National Headquarters, Philippine National Police, Camp Crame, Quezon City (1999), p. 2. The document is marked D1, classified as secret. The document also refers to MILF's links with al-Qaeda and MaK stating that, "A certain Zine el Abiddin Abou Zoubaida of Maktab al Khidmat has been in contact with 2 prominent personalities of the MILF." Zoubaida was, of course, a Saudi on the leadership council of *al-Qaeda*.

52. Quoted in Maria Ressa, "Infiltrating the MILF," *Newsbreak*, October 27, 2002, at http://www.newsbreak.ph/2002/10/27/infiltrating-the-milf/ (accessed July 14, 2004).

53. Philippines Directorate for Intelligence, "Reference Folder on International Terrorism," pp. 1-2.

54. Ibid., p. 2. The Philippine police report concluded: "Bin Laden and Khalifa are channelling funds to support the MILF through its various Islamic NGOs. The MILF on the other hand provided training venues for other Islamic extremists in their stronghold areas."

55. See Zachary Abuza, *Funding Terrorism Research in Southeast Asia: The Financial Network of Al Qaeda and Jemaah Islamiyah* (Washington: The National Bureau of Asian Research, 2003).

56. "Dancing Girls and Romance on Road to Terrorist Attacks," *Sydney Morning Herald*, June 25, 2002.

57. Laurie Mylroie, "The World Trade Center Bomb: Who is Ramzi Yousef? And Why It Matters," *National Interest* (Winter, 1995/96). "The Baluch Connection: Is Khalid Sheikh Mohammed tied to Bagdad?" *Wall Street Journal*, March 18, 2003.

58. See "Top al-Qaeda Suspect Captured," *BBC News*, March 1, 2003 at http://www.bbc.co.uk/1/hi/world/south_asia/2811473.stm (accessed February 24, 2003).

59. See Christopher Kremmer, "Then There Were Two: Al Qaeda Planner Caught," *Sydney Morning Herald*, March 3, 2003.

60. "Al Qaeda Planned to Kill Pope: Report," *San Francisco Examiner*, November 11, 2002.

61. Myrolie, "The Baluch Connection."

62. Jessica Stern, "The Protean Enemy," *Foreign Affairs*, July/August 2003 available at

http://jessicastern.files.wordpress.com/2010/05/the-protean-enemy_foreign-affairs_julyaugust-2003.pdf , p. 31 (accessed February 28, 2011).

63. See Thomas M. Kiefer, *The Tausug Violence and Law in a Philippine Moslem Society* (New York: Holt, Rinehart and Winston, 1972), pp. 35-36.

64. See Eduardo F. Ugarte "The Alliance System of the Abu Sayyaf, 1993-2000," *Studies in Conflict and Terrorism*, Vol. 31, No. 2 (2008), p. 134.

65. Noor Huda Ismail, 'The Role of kinship in Jemaah Islamiah," *Straits Times*, April 22, 2006.

66. Zachary Abuza, "Terror Network Spreads," *The Australian*, October 9, 2006.

67. "Saudi Linked Charity Linked to Bali Bombs," *The Australian*, August 8, 2006.

68. "Al Qaeda Plot to Bomb US Ships Foiled by MI6," *Daily Telegraph*, January 13, 2002.

69. "PM Reveals Plan to Crash Jet into Changi," *Sunday Times* (Singapore), April 7, 2002.

70. Rahim, "White Paper Sheds Light on Singapore JI Indoctrination Process."

71. See Mark Baker, "Evidence Points to Web of Extremists," *The Age*, November 9, 2002.

72. See "Confessions of an al-Qaeda Terrorist," *Time Magazine*, September 15, 2002.

73. "A Deadly Connection," *Sydney Morning Herald*, November 16, 2002.

74. "Four Corners: The Bali Confessions—Chronology," at http://www.abc.net.au/4corners/content/2003/20030210_bali_confessions/chronology.htm (accessed October 10, 2004).

75. See Seth Mydans, "Suspect Going on Trial in Bali Blast," *International Herald Tribune*, May 12, 2003.

76. Marian Wilkinson, "We'll Hit You: Pre-Bali Alert," *Sydney Morning Herald*, October 16, 2002.

77. *The Australian*, January 25-26, 2003.

78. *The Australian*, February 15-16, 2003.

79. Jusuf Wanandi, "Indonesia: A Failed State?" *The Washington Quarterly*, Vol. 25, No. 3 (Summer 2002), p. 142.

80. Alan Dupont, quoted in *Far Eastern Economic Review*, October 2, 2002.

81. Reme Ahmed, "Asean Ministers Acknowledge Defining Terrorism is Not Crucial, Fighting it is," *Straits Times*, May 21, 2002.

82. See David Martin Jones and M.L.R. Smith, "Making Process, Not Progress: ASEAN and the Evolving East Asian Regional Order," *International Security*, Vol. 32, No. 1 (Summer 2007), pp. 170-174.

83. See for example, Dini Djalal, "Asia's Intelligence Gap," *Foreign Policy* (March/April 2003).

84. See "Bali Opens Terror Trial in Blast Fatal to 200," *International Herald Tribune*, May 12, 2002.

85. See Caroline Munro, "Bashir Goes on Trial," *The Daily Telegraph* (Australia) May 11, 2002.

86. Quoted in letter sent to President Bush from Bashir, *The Australian*, September 2, 2003.

87. International Crisis Group, *Jemaah Islamiyah in South East Asia: Damaged but still dangerous*, ICG Asia Report 63, Jakarta/Brussels, August 26, 2003, p. 1.

88. Quoted in *Weekend Australian*, August 23-24, 2003, p. 6.

89. Zachary Abuza, "Fall of the Teflon Terrorist? Jemaah Islamiah and the Arrest of Abu Bakar Bashir," *Australia Israel Review*, September 2010, pp. 12-15.

90. *Weekend Australian*, August 14-15, 2010, p. 22. See also *DailyTelegraph*, December 13, 2010.

91. Wahyudi Seriaatmadja, "Militant Jailed for 14 Years for Role in Aceh Training Camp," *Straits Times*, January 21, 2011.

92. See Mark Baker, "Angry Thais Threaten Writers Over Hambali Plot Reports," *Sydney Morning Herald*, November 14, 2002. See also "Into the Heart of Darkness," *The Age*, November 16, 2002.

93. Zachary Abuza, "Umar Patek: Indonesia's Most Wanted,"*Militant Leadership Monitor*, Vol. 1, No. 3, March 31, 2010, p. 1.

94. Author interview with Tito M. Karnavian, International Centre for Political Violence and Terrorism Research, S. Rajaratnam School of International Studies, Nanyang Technological University, Singapore, June 13, 2007.

95. See Jones and Smith, "The Perils of Hyper-Vigilance," pp. 43-48.

96. *Terrorism in Southeast Asia: The Threat and Response*, Report of an International Conference organized by the Institute of Defence and Strategic Studies and Office of the Coordinator for Counterterrorism, US Department of State, Washington, DC, Singapore, April 12-13, 2006.

97. Author interview, June 2007.

98. Author interview: Tito M. Karnavian further observed, ironically we think, that the practice of de-radicalization of former JI members involved, "when they cooperate we give them a carrot and when they don't we give them the stick."

99. *Terrorism in Southeast Asia: The Threat and Response*.

100. David Kilcullen, "Subversion and Counter-subversion in the Campaign Against Terrorism in Europe," *Studies in Conflict and Terrorism*, Vol. 20, No.8 (2008), p. 652.

101. Gunaratna, "Ideology in Terrorism," p. 95.

102. Goh Chok Tong, "After Amman: Uniting to Defeat Terrorism—Speech by Senior Minister Goh Chok Tong at the Opening Ceremony of East-West Dialogue on 16 Nov 05," Singapore, Ministry of Foreign Affairs Press Release, http://app.mfa.gov.sg/pr/read_content.asp?View,4387, (accessed May 12, 2010).

103. Wong Kan Seng, "Guarding Against Radical Ideology," in Kader, *Fighting Terrorism*, p.20

104. Goh, "After Amman."

105. Yaacob Ibrahim, "Stand up to Deviants: Don't Give Them the Last Word," in Kader, *Fighting Terrorism*.

106. Mohamed Feisal bin Mohamed Hussein, "The Role of the Religious Rehabilitation Group in Singapore," in Kader, *Fighting Terrorism*, p. 166.

107. Zakir Hussain, "Reforming JI Detainees Remains a Long Struggle," *Straits Times*, February 3, 2007.

108. M.H.Bin Hassan 'Imam Samudra's Justification for the Bali Bombing', *Studies in Conflict and Terrorism*, Vol. 30, No. 12 (2007), p. 1051.

109. Ibid., p. 1052.

Contributors

JACK BARCLAY
is a strategic communications advisor based in the United Kingdom.

DAVID MARTIN JONES
is Associate Professor in the School of Political Science and
International Studies, University of Queensland.

ISMAIL KHAN
is an independent scholar and writer based in Pakistan.

HASSAN MNEIMNEH
is Senior Transatlantic Fellow for MENA and the Islamic World
at the German Marshall Fund.

APARNA PANDE
is a research fellow at Hudson Institute.

M.L.R. SMITH
is Professor of Strategic Theory, Department of War Studies,
King's College, University of London.

SAMUEL TADROS
is a research fellow at Hudson Institute, and a senior partner
with the Egyptian Union for Liberal Youth.